Everything You Need To Know About
EMOTIONS

Everything You Need To Know About EMOTIONS

The only introduction you'll ever need to understand emotions

Lygya Barreto, Ph.D.

Writer's Showcase
San Jose New York Lincoln Shanghai

Everything You Need To Know About EMOTIONS

Writer's Showcase
an imprint of iUniverse, Inc.

For information address:
iUniverse, Inc.
5220 S. 16th St., Suite 200
Lincoln, NE 68512
www.iuniverse.com

ISBN: 0-595-24698-2

Printed in the United States of America

Dedicated to:

Beings of all cultures, backgrounds, planets and dimensions I dedicate these lines to the power of communication
Between all of us in the universe

With special gratitude to the ones closest to me in this lifetime:

Eunice Leite, mother
Nilton Leite, stepfather

David Chin, best friend and supporter

Aurelito S. T. Barreto, biological father

♥

"THE POWER OF EMOTIONS IS IN EVERYTHING WE
CHOOSE TO DO"

Contents

INTRODUCTION

I wanted to write a book that would serve as a wake-up call to many. I have seen so many of us in total turmoil because of lack of knowledge on the subject of emotions. Often I felt that society in general focuses attention on the physical, spiritual and mental levels of healing, ignoring the emotional level. These efforts at theoretical and analytical thinking do not allow us to explore the core of our unpleasant feelings, such as depression.

Many of us use work as a drug to distract ourselves from problems. Others become addicted to drugs, chocolate, TV, shopping, compulsive eating, insomnia, cigarette smoking, etc. No matter what the behavior is, the addiction is there and the distractions divert our attention from the deep trauma and hurt we went through as children and young adults.

The fact that many clients came to me frustrated and approaching hopelessness after many unproductive sessions of clinical psychology, also inspired me to write this book. I believe every clinical psychologist should have alternative modalities of healing on their agenda. Moreover, universities should require courses in alternative modalities in addition to the conventional psychology curriculum. That way, more people would be helped by natural means.

It is known in the alternative healing community that no one "heals" anyone. The client is healed by his or her own willpower. In this field, there are wonderful people many call "healers," but I prefer to call them "devoted and powerful guides." Clearly, one must follow his or her higher self-guidance and be aware of those operating dishonestly and exploiting our trust. Listening to our internal warning signals is vital to our survival. We must develop animal instincts and intuition. Not by coincidence, there are guides for this very purpose, working to help us develop these abilities every second of our existence.

I have been guiding many clients in regaining their own power and it feels great to me to be able to do so. It shows that I accumulate enough power to share with others. In my point of view, we cannot give what we do not have. Most of us had our powers taken in our early years by peers and family programming. As children, we were hypnotized by our families to think and act as they would like. We grow up with our parents' belief systems, trusting that they are good for us. Some of us eventually wake up to our own dreams and belief systems, which inspires us to fight for our mission. But sadly, the majority of us do not wake up. We continue to live our lives following someone else's dream. We must search for help in order to break the patterns and cycles of guilt, lack of self-esteem, anger, lack of self-love, etc.

This book is a spiritual and energetic, not scientific, approach to this fascinating and powerful subject. I have been reading about intellectual approaches to the subject of emotions in many books and articles, but every time this subject is touched, words get in the way of simplicity.

I chose to write a book that would make sense to an eight—as well as to an 80-year old, whatever their rational mind background, IQ or degree. Something anyone could read and understand about which emotions are influencing their lives, how they came to be and how to proceed in safeguarding a productive emotional life.

This book is a service to you who are seeking general emotional knowledge along with mental guidance, spiritual evolution, physical awareness and emotional healing.

Use this book to learn more about yourself and about how to start to release the stagnating emotions that prevent you from experiencing happiness and moving forward toward your goals in life.

Enjoy _

STATEMENT OF A HEALER

As a healer I feel the power of my dimensional connections.
I see awesome miracles of healing take place
in peoples' minds, bodies, spirit and emotions.
I have been in their shoes for quite some time...
Now I am living proof of the transformational
and powerful phenomenon of the force of our willpower
on the choices we make.

As a role model I speak
I am assertive
I am secure
I am mature
That is who I became
and who I am...

1

WHAT IS EMOTION?

The Oxford English Dictionary defines the word, "emotion" as, "…any agitation or disturbance of mind, feeling, passion; any exciting mental state." Some theorists call the word a term; some say it denotes distinctive thoughts, psychological or biological states and a range of propensities to act.

The word "emotion" comes from the Latin verb "to move" with the prefix "e" to connote "move away".

I prefer to simplify the definition in one word, saying it is "ENERGY." We are made of energy and so are emotions. EMOTION IS THE ENERGY THAT GUIDES US TO DO EVERYTHING! IT IS OUR MOST POWERFUL ENERGETIC DEVICE.

Think about it….
They can start war and they can start love. They can make us ill and they can make us healthy, and our history is the history of our emotions, as well as our own personal story!

What do you think Emotions are? Normally we talk about the way we feel, but never talk about this important subject in depth, the way we should.

I DON'T KNOW ANYTHING THAT IS MORE IMPORTANT IN LIFE THAN THE WAY WE FEEL. Isn't it interesting how we take for granted important things in our lives every day?

Emotion is live energy.

Therefore, it is everything around us, including ourselves.
As everything that is energetic, it must flow.
This flow of energetic charge, just like light and electricity, will allow us to experience this wonderful process. If we don't allow it, it will explode eventually, somehow.

Even though nature was created to help us, some of us control this wonderful tool, blocking this charge until we die…

Emotion produces motion and motion produces emotion.

Emotions are vital to our existence, and we cannot allow ourselves to detach from them. There are literally millions of people out there who feel almost dead inside…literally afraid to feel anything for fear of getting hurt once again, in some way.

In most cases, it's all about fear due to things that have happened in our lives while we were growing up. Sometimes it's an existential fear, caused just by the fact that no one really knows the answers to why we're here. Why were we born into the families we're in? Why do we live in the city we live in, with the people we're involved with, or in the circumstances in which we find ourselves?

It's time to allow ourselves to feel what we're meant to feel—our beautiful range of emotions. It's a great experience if we allow them to be open; always remembering that fear is the opposite of faith. Where our faith is strong, there is no room for fear in our lives, and so, as we learn this process, we learn to accept and honor our emotions the way it should be.

We learn to let our emotions shine like the bright stars they are, purely for the sake of putting out positive energy to the Universe, and for the evolution of our higher levels of consciousness.

The majority of people prefer to try to detach from their emotions and to ignore them altogether. (Do you know what the word "try" means? It means not there, not here—just in between. This is no place to be. Either we do or we don't!) This attempt at detachment results in the development of physical and emotional blocks. It literally causes disease.

The word "disease" itself is made up of two parts: "dis" and "ease"—literally meaning "a lack of ease." That's exactly what happens when we get sick. The part of the body that is ill is lacking in Universal Life Force, caused by our blocking, or not being in touch with, our emotions, and our refusal to allow our Universal Life Force to flow freely to all parts of our bodies. Some of the most common illnesses linked to this process are back pain, shoulder and neck pain, jaw pain, headaches, allergies, asthma, depression, phobias, chronic fatigue, and even cancer.

A good exercise is to write down the emotion that gives you the most trouble—meaning an emotion that is the hardest for you to handle, for whatever reason. Did you ever feel controlled by one of your emotions, instead of allowing it to be expressed easily?

Whatever it is—anger, fear, lust, happiness, or rage—write it down, with an explanation. After writing it, search for its roots in your childhood. Go into it with brutal honesty, for your own sake. Find out why you keep feeling the way you do, over and over throughout your life, and bring that same feeling into your present. Analyze and feel that emotion with full intent—don't save anything. If you want to scream—go for it! If you want to cry—go for it! If you want to go wild, go for it! Allow yourself to "feel" deeply for the first time, without any control in the least.

Have you noticed that your most disturbing emotions are like a double-edged sword? They can either work for you or against you. They can be either your greatest dream or your worst nightmare.

See how many of you can relate to this: You find someone you think you might want to be in a relationship with; which is not a strange thing in itself, right? To want to be in a relationship with someone else is a basic human need, right? But how come many of us actually feel ourselves going into a cold sweat, just at the prospect of even calling that person, in trying to tell them how we feel, or even just thinking about doing that?

How many of us create our own movie in our heads, projecting the worst possible outcome, before anything has even happened? Most of us are famous for doing that. Suddenly, in the space of a few seconds, we all become Steven Spielberg. We create scenarios, cast them, direct them, act them out and then we shoot the movie—and even worse—we believe it! We run this make-believe movie through our minds and we think it's real.

I knew a lonely man; the kind of guy who could see an attractive woman standing across the street waiting for a bus, and before he even said, "Hello," in his mind he went through 30 years of marriage, and it ended badly. That's called projection, and it's what we tend to do.

It's really all about fear. We project an outcome that is based in fear, and not in reality, because we are afraid to experience our true emotions. The funny thing is, until we learn how to own our emotions and the power that goes with them, this continues to happen throughout our lives, no matter how old we get. We make the same mistakes over and over again. There's this great definition of the word "insanity" that I love. It says, "Insanity is doing the same things over and over again, always expecting different results."

How many of us can relate to that? We find certain patterns in our lives that seem to recur over and over again, and we think to ourselves, 'How can this be happening to me again? What's the matter with me?

Won't I ever learn?' In order to break the pattern, we must learn about our emotions and how to handle them so that we own them, use them to guide us, use them as tools—not the other way around.

In order to change the outcome of events, we have to change what we do, and change is scary to a lot of people—just as scary as feeling our emotions. Just remember, if you keep on doing what you always did, you'll keep on getting what you always got. Change is critical.

Emotion is the energy that guides us to do everything.

2

WHY EMOTION WAS CREATED

Emotion was created to defend us, to help us to release energy in relation to actions and situations.

It was created to help us to realize we are alive. It will always be there for us to use, to process, learn and find. If we don't use it we will die inside.

Nothing will matter if we don't realize that feelings are a wonderful friend for us, either to lean on and cry, or laugh about anything, to survive...

So go ahead and feel it. Whatever is there to feel, it's nature, it's real. Don't deny it. Be truthful with yourself and others so you can be healed.

The purposes of our Emotions are:

—to help us to react
—to help us to produce actions
—to release energy and attract energy
—to guide and teach us
—to protect us
—to help us to choose and make decisions
—help us to connect to others
—to help us to evolve

—to help us to connect with other dimensions, higher self and Consciousness

To learn the purpose of our emotions, we must allow them to guide us. We must feel deeply and react in a positive manner. In other words, when we feel an emotion as a result of action, we just react naturally as it flows, without judgment or control. If we do just that, we will see that we will not have to react with the usual uncomfortable sensations, because it will have become normal for us to just react.

If we manage to react to the right person, to the right degree, at the right time, for the right purpose, and in the right way—we accomplish maturity at last. The person who provoked the reaction will learn from it, and we will also. The lessons can vary.

If we take life experience from a spiritual perspective, we will be able to see our problems as opportunities to increase our understanding of the deeper meaning of life and our true purpose.

If you're still debating about this or think it's too hard to change your life for the better, picture yourself as a baby. One day, out of nowhere, you decided to walk for the first time. If you don't remember, observe a baby taking that walk. There is nothing to stop the baby; she or he just goes for it, without anyone telling them, 'Okay, today you are going to practice your walk.' What about talking? Similarly, adults may insist on saying, 'Goo goo, gaa gaa' to us, but still we keep going for the most difficult words.

Does it take a while? Yes. Do we do it anyway, not giving up on ourselves? Yes! Why can't we decide, at an adult age, to make the decision to be happy, with the same assurance of our natural desire to grow? The only difference is that when we are young, we don't analyze at all, we just go for it. And notice the happiness on the baby's face when it finally accomplishes that goal…That could be your face, if you decide to become happy. Even if takes a while, just keep on working on it, just like when you were a baby. It's nothing new. You've always had the power to make that decision to change your life. Wake up! You've got the power!

Your future depends on you, nobody else.

3

THE IMPACT OF OUR FIRST EMOTIONAL STAGE

There are four bodies in a human life in this dimension: the physical, mental, spiritual and emotional. In the first stage of our lives, we learn that our physical body is hungry and needs food. We start to walk, we fall, we learn to run, and we think we can fly. Our physical body is our world and we think we can do everything we imagine.

In the second stage, our mental body starts to develop. It begins to think and grow curious. We start speaking, ask questions, and become analytical. In the third stage, we get in touch with morality and spirituality, and may be raised in religious practice, according to our parents' beliefs. Finally, our emotions begin to take shape, according to the way we are raised and educated. This is when many traumas occur and we are taught how to "control" our emotions.

The first stage determines the shape and support of our emotions for the rest of our lives in this dimension. Depending on what happens in this stage, we will be successful business people or not, depressed or not, overweight or not, allergic or not, have healthy romantic relationships or not, and so on…

SCIENCE says that our brain is divided into two parts or two minds: the analytical mind and the emotional mind.

I think the analytical mind grows forever, as long as we have life to learn, our analytical intellect will learn lessons with our experiences. On the other hand, the EMOTIONAL mind won't grow any more than 10 years old. I don't have scientific proof of my statement; I just have life experience, intuition and a great amount of sense to support my statement. This is how I came to this conclusion.

As we grow older, we learn a tremendous array of things and we learn analytically what is right or wrong to do. Even when we are dying we are leaning what it is to die. Maturity will come when we have sufficient experiences in life. But this does not happen on the emotional side at all. The same emotion we feel when we are three years old is the same feeling when we are 30 or 70. Sadness is sadness, whether we are nine or 90. What changes is our way of thinking about a situation, not the level of our FEELING. We can try to control or suppress our feeling as we mature, but the feeling will stay on the same energy level from the day we were born to the day we die.

We keep the unpleasant and emotional childhood experiences intact in our subconscious minds until we mature enough to find out that something is wrong and that we cannot deal with it by ourselves. Some of us choose to change that pattern; some of us won't. Many of us become depressed, sad and rebellious (full of anger) in our teen cycle, getting into drugs, cigarettes and plenty of trouble. If our willpower doesn't develop strongly enough, we carry on our denials and sabotage ourselves for this entire life cycle.

Many of us, as adults in this society, became workaholics, in a strong effort to distract ourselves from the emotional problems we carry within our subconscious. Good examples are: the ladies' man; sex addicts, and men and women who like to have many lovers, in the illusion that they are creating "power" on the conscious level. They are actually desperately looking for love and attention.

There can be also anger in this process, to a point of extreme denial of their true feelings; "defending" themselves from commitment, so they won't suffer rejection as they did in childhood.

Childhood > control > program > belief system > fear

4

WHY WE CONTROL OUR EMOTIONS AND WHY WE SHOULDN'T

The primary reason we control our emotions is because of fear. In our early age, our parents, teachers or others, influenced us to do so. To be strong was the same as to control our emotions, and we "believed" in this theory. This not only caused us to sabotage ourselves indefinitely, but also initiated unwanted patterns.

Most people prefer to control emotions rather than to feel, and then release them, forever. These individuals are afraid to feel. I know many people who avoid the emotional pain by taking legal drugs. It serves the purpose for a while. But the truth is that those individuals are not dealing with the root of their problems; they are just touching the surface with the sedatives they take.

It is an illusion to think that drugs are going to take the pain away. The drug effect will be momentary and could (in most cases) aggravate the physical body even moreso with side effects, and, later on, with a feeling of weakness. The drugs will produce limited effects and eventually an addiction will take place. That person is not taking charge of their life using their own willpower to overcome their traumas. That fact alone will cause the person to enter a cycle of depression with no improvement in their self-esteem issues.

Some people become aware of these patterns and make efforts to end this process, others don't even know, consciously, that something is wrong. Others prefer to have a laid-back attitude, feeling sorry for themselves.

Millions of people fail to think for themselves and become slaves to the opinions of others due to early-age traumas. A lot of us are afraid of being judged by society if we allow our emotions to show.

We should all know the importance of the influence of emotions in our physical, mental and spiritual "bodies." Because they are connected for a purpose, we cannot afford to neglect the one we most fear and run way from—our Emotional body.

Most of us, in order to "protect ourselves" from past traumas, play a game between the subconscious and the conscious mind. We keep the hurt (emotion) in the subconscious mind, (I call it "the little box") and act with the conscious mind, as if we no longer remember past experiences. That way, we think we are avoiding trouble, and keep on avoiding it, until our physical, mental and existential lives begin to send us messages. These may come in the form of diseases, unwanted patterns, dreams, bad humor, unreasonable anger, etc…If we don't take action, our other bodies begin to deteriorate as a result, and our connection with the natural health flux of life, becomes foreign to us.

For the masses, true healing should consider all of the parts of the whole and deal with the source of the problem, rather than relieving only the symptoms. Only those who have mental and physical disorders should take drugs, since they "cannot" control themselves.

The subconscious mind never forgets. It keeps taking us to the same patterns that caused the blockages. This process reminds us to deal with, and learn from, the trauma, until it cleanses the old and allows the new to come. Once our consciousness (mental body) learns about this, we can no longer afford to put aside our unfinished energetic flow.

Emotions were created to react to an action and release it. If we don't release it, we block the natural flow of energy that's supposed to take place. To experience full happiness in this lifetime we must "recognize" the need of emotional release and change.

Once I suggested a client close her eyes and think of a situation in which she could see herself happy, making lots of money, with a harmonious romantic relationship. She immediately reacted, saying, 'How can I visualize that I am happy, when I am sick?' I told her that like the crystal in front of her that was solidified energy, we are also energetic beings, therefore we can also solidify our thoughts. Just as all the objects in the world were, at some point, only in the creator's mind, eventually becoming materialized. She also could, and must, give thought to the opportunity of materializing her dreams.

I believe that problems were created to challenge us to grow clever, sharper, smarter…Problems were created for us to find the solutions and then to let them go, learn from them, and treasure the guidance to a better purpose and accomplishment.

How many times do we find the solution to a problem and feel proud of doing so…This should be the case all of the time. Our brain is so incredibly awesome, that WE CAN FIND SOLUTIONS FOR LIT-ERALLY EVERYTHING!

Now picture the person who chooses to use the problem as her or his companion (which is my mother's case by the way…) This person will suffer, and whine, get depressed, complain and nag, and eventually get sick. My mother has had surgery seven times and literally, every week goes to a different doctor. No matter what I say, she's still going to go through her pattern every day.

My grandmother committed suicide for the same reason. I use their example to take care of my life in the highest level of positive energy, every single second of my life—got it? We can take a lemon and make lemonade anytime we desire.

We have to become conscious of what the problem is and how it is affecting us. The key to change is "awareness." Don't forget that we keep the unpleasant childhood emotional experiences intact in our subconscious mind.

In the process, a good way to start to heal emotionally is to take a new look at emotions.

Action > emotion > reaction > action > emotion

5

THE IMPORTANCE OF EMOTIONAL GUIDANCE

There is nothing more important in life than the way we feel!

We have wars because of Emotions and at the same time we have love because of Emotions.

The importance of emotions in our lives is vital—without them we wouldn't have passion, wisdom, love, attraction, excitement and (why not?)—drama!

Our emotions provide guidance in the learning process of our existence. They are elemental. We do things in this existence for two reasons:

1. To avoid pain (emotion)
2. To gain pleasure (emotion)

Avoiding pain is a defense mechanism we all have and use, one way or the other, in our lives. Without this mechanism, we could not be raised and educated the way we have been. We would not fear dangerous situations or punishment. But sometimes, we get carried away with our defenses and go to extreme measures in protection, particularly against the emotions. In that case, the results also can be extreme.

For example, take the person with chronic fatigue syndrome or depression, who is confined, with no social life. Or, on the other hand, take the person who is never home, who is always partying and distracting themselves from something. They have a possessive relationship or no romantic relationship at all; excessive sex or no sex at all. They may be addicted to such things as drugs, alcohol, and cigarettes, TV, nostalgia, chocolate, or other sugars. They may be workaholics, shopaholics, overeaters, or they may not eat at all.

To seek pleasure is a healthy and necessary, natural course in life. But sometimes we get carried away and go to extremes with pleasure or punishment. As we can see, the process is almost the same, whether we are depriving or overindulging ourselves. But we cannot go wrong in dealing, at once, with those emotions that target our behavior, so that we can use our protection and pleasurable instincts in a healthy and balanced way.

When we finally become aware that we are doing something compulsively, we can start to move into the process of working on it. It's a hard road and requires a lot of persistence and willpower. But once we find the cause, we feel relieved and proud for overcoming that particular compulsive tendency.

As pain is a good guide for us because it teaches us in the long-run, so is pleasure. Just as yin and yang complement one another, pain and pleasure serve the same purpose. Again, it's up to us to determine the actions that will bring us balance and fulfillment. If we realize that we are doing too much either to avoid pain or gain pleasure, it's time to reflect. It's time to take a serious, mature, look at our patterns.

Think with reason and total respect for yourself in the actions that you decide to take on your path. Every little thing counts; we owe it to ourselves to work on not taking our existence for granted. Treat yourself like you would treat a beautiful baby, newly born, with all the care and attention your inner child deserves. Be careful if you see yourself habitually forgetting about it or procrastinating; that is self-abandonment, and it shows where your priorities are. Eventually those choices will catch up with you.

Everything is positive in the end. There will be always a positive lesson to be learned no matter what. We must appreciate "all" emotions for all the messages they bring. They help us to learn about ourselves and others. They are the best guides of our existence.

"It's from our emotions that all our decisions are made, all our actions are taken, and from all actions is where all the results of our lives come from."

Anthony Robbins

Life > energy > motion > emotion

6

OUR RESPONSIBILITY REGARDING EMOTIONS

It is our responsibility to know about ourselves, in order to be able to know others, even those very close to us, such as our own babies and/or lovers. If we don't know ourselves, we cannot, and will not, know other beings deeply. Once we know why and how our emotions were shaped, we will be able to master the true Self that is here for a reason and needs to feed on emotion in this existence. We must allow the real Self to emerge and to blossom as it should. Only then are we going to find out what's here on this planet for us to do. All that is around us is a reflection of us; we attract the energy around us because we have the energetic power to do so.

Everything we build has to come from within first. We must get clear on ourselves, in order to relate to the world in a successful and clear manner.

A lot of us take very good care of other people and have been sympathetic to other people's problems, with the good excuse that we are good human beings. But if we overdo it, we are using them to forget about our own problems. In fact, we are, in many cases, relating only to that problem and distracting ourselves from our own. I am not saying one should not help others—I am saying HELP YOURSELF IN ORDER TO HELP OTHERS. When we receive instructions on an airplane, they read: "Put the oxygen mask on you first and then on your child," because if you die, you cannot save your child. This is the same way it is on your emotional journey.

Our knowledge is always increasing through our actions, and those actions must be impeccable with ourselves first, in order to provide to others the same level of honesty and to serve as good examples, as well. Most of the time, the simple fact that you take good care of yourself, attracts the curiosity of friends, neighbors and even strangers, with questions about your health—'What do you do to look so good, or to be so happy?' or, 'How can you keep up?' etc…

We are, indeed, the best promotional ad there is to help others. If I don't have good health, how can I teach about it? If I don't know about love, how can I talk about it with certainty?

To make sense and help others, we must take the responsibility of knowledge about SELF. I suggest books, seminars, workshops, videos and holistic magazines. The health food stores are packed with free holistic magazines filled with information about various modalities of healing. Nothing is an overwhelming problem if we focus on the solutions instead—and believe it—there will be always a solution for a problem. Nothing is negative if we see it as positive—and believe it—there will be always two sides for us to examine. There are always two sides of the coin: the yin and yang, night and day, black and white. It is really up to us to make the decision which side to take.

Once we learn how to see life from both sides, to take charge of our lives and work on our willpower, fighting for our evolutionary journey—only then are we on our way to real freedom. Our emotions become our friends, instead of the enemy. We no longer judge ourselves or, consequently, others. (We have to work very hard on that one.) We begin to focus on what motivates us the most. Nothing, I repeat, nothing, will stop you from accomplishing what you came here to accomplish.

To acknowledge our emotions means to show respect, be alert, observe, and react. Blocking our emotions conscientiously, like most humans do, we block, also, the process of learning why we are here. That is why we must observe our actions with care, as we would observe the most important process there is.

I knew a woman who got to her apartment and saw that the door was open. Her heart began to beat really fast, but she still walked into the apartment, where a man was robbing the place. Unfortunately, she was raped as a result of that action. I asked her why she hadn't run out of there, since she felt something was wrong. She said she thought she was invulnerable.

My example here is: the emotion of fear is good for warning. If she would have just listened to her heart, she would have saved herself of from great harm.

Know how to use your emotions to your advantage, not to your destruction. Defenses were created to protect us, but it's is up to us to use them in the right way. Get smarter about them! Don't take them for granted.

It is our responsibility to know ourselves in order to know others.

Action > emotion > acknowledge > respect > alert > observe > react

7

EMOTIONS & NATURE

I like to compare the four most commonly recognized feelings with the four elements of nature, because it helps us to see the direct influence of these elements on the way we feel.

Fear = Earth, Happiness = Air, Sadness = Water, Anger = Fire

Let's start with FEAR. Many people want to stop being afraid, because they think that fear is holding them back; stopping them from accomplishing at new levels in life. It's okay to feel more confident and courageous, but, like everything else, fear needs to be respected as part of our experience. It's there because it is necessary to be there—to protect us against disaster. For example, when something is very hot, your body will contract in reaction, to keep you from getting hurt. Fear will warn us a dangerous situation is approaching.

In short, the feeling of fear is necessary in many occasions in our lives. It's up to us to learn how to balance this feeling at the right time, and in the right situation. To learn from fear is to be courageous, not weak, like some of us learned to think.

HAPPINESS is the best medicine there is. Only an optimistic person can and will experience life with happiness. Sometimes we are so seriously dedicated to our responsibilities that we forget to have fun and honor our happiness for being alive, health, in love etc. We can and should be more serious about living happily for the sake of freedom and enlightenment.

It is extremely important that we include happiness in our day-to-day lives and schedules. Think about the things that you enjoy, that make you laugh or feel childish. We must do at least one fun thing every day or change to the positive and humorous ways of seeing things.

SADNESS is the feeling that helps us to release blockages. That's why we cry when we are sad. The tears serve as water, cleansing our pain and suffering. After a good cry, we feel relieved and calmer, whatever the situation is. Maybe it doesn't always go away right way, but we feel better afterwards, without a doubt.

Many people, particularly males, think that crying in public, or even by oneself, is a sign of weakness; that if you control your crying, that means you're strong. What occur as a result, are emotional blockages. Consequently, they will explode in a different form, such as physical disease. (Derivatives of sadness are depression, chronic fatigue syndrome, etc.)

ANGER is a very common feeling. We feel anger when someone does wrong or something goes wrong. Frustration and indignation take over. Our nervous system gets fired up and we explode like a volcano, or we try to control the anger for one reason or another. If we control it for a long time, our liver will become more and more diseased as we mature, as the liver is the organ that keeps anger inside. Because the liver functions as the filter for all that we take into our bodies, the result is pretty obvious: disease will attack again.

Releasing our blockages will enable us to be open to emotional energy, which can be utilized in positive and productive ways.

8

THE EMOTIONAL BODY WE CARRY INSIDE THE PHYSICAL BODY

We have three bodies that have three distinct mechanisms. One body is the dense physical body, where the organs are sustained with food and water. This body is the "box" in which we carry the second body, which people from many religions call the "soul."

A good comparison is that between water's various ways of existing and our body layers. We can see water in big oceans and rivers, when its particles are connected in great number. But water is also made of vapor (where we see it in the form of steam or fog, but cannot touch it) and also in solid form, such as ice.

It's the same with us. We have the physical that we can see, and our other dimensions that we can only sense, talk to, and see in dreams and/or visions. We finally discard the physical when we die. There are additional bodies that serve to make us whole. For example, the mental body promotes thinking, creativity, rationality, ethics, etc. But I'm going to focus on the emotional body, to keep it simple. I love simple things.

The emotional body carries all our emotions and can be detached while we sleep. It is responsible for our adventures in our dreamtime and can be consciously projected out of our body. Some mediums and clairvoyant people know how to execute this paranormal phenomenon as second nature, in order to see the past, present, future and other lives.

For a better understanding of this process, consider these examples: When we feel like we're falling, before or after sleeping, that's the soul leaving or returning to the body energetically. We have daydreams oftentimes. That happens when our emotional body is detached. We may be talking to friends, watching TV, or reading a book, but we're still navigating la-la land.

What about dreams? As we all know, that's another time when we "feel," "see," "smell," "hear" and "taste." We are definitely there; to the point where we can sometimes wake up sweating, our hearts pumping really hard, so vivid was the dream or nightmare. Sometimes we can remember our dreams, sometimes not, but be assured we all work in other dimensions in our dreamtime. Another example of detachment of the soul from the physical is the sensation we have when we are ready to wake up or stop the dream we are having, and kind of panic when we see that our physical body is not moving despite our efforts. It seems that our mind is working, but our body is not responding. (That's because our soul, or psychosoma, is still not entirely there.

It is possible to consciously send your soul to another dimension and have lucidity in another dimension as well. There are institutions dedicated to this particular phenomenon. If you feel curious about it, take a look at my references at the end of this article.

If we owe it to ourselves to take good care of our physical bodies, we owe, also, the commitment to know, and to take better care of, our other bodies as well, so that we can became whole.

It's important to know about the theory that our emotional body carries all of the memories of this and other lifetime experiences, and that until we deal with those issues, we won't fly free.

Another note of importance: the chakras act as intermediaries between the two bodies and the channels responsible for the process of energetic emotional charges. The literal translation of "chakra" is "focal point, gateway, or the way in and out."

Finally, our soul, or psychosoma, is in touch with, and is being watched by "helpers," whom people from many religions call "angels" or "guides." Some of you won't believe in this theory and that's okay with me, but who do you think you talking to every single moment of your life, inside of your head, hmm? You must know that somebody else is listening as you're talking all the time and getting your questions answered. What about your signals, intuitions, gut feelings and dreams? What do you think all those signs are about? Have you ever stopped talking when you are alone?

9

WHAT EMOTIONAL TRAUMA MEANS TO OUR EXISTENTIAL GROWTH

When we are traumatized in any period in our lives, our subconscious minds never forget. Some of us manage to produce amnesia so we won't remember on the conscious level at all.

To allow our emotions to help us, including the combating of self-corruption or sabotage, we transform our personalities into catalyzing agents for the evolution of others. The understanding of the power of our consciousness, the rational organization of our own ideas, expressed in our personal work, will lead us to ultimate freedom and happiness.

Millions of people comprise the unthinking human masses: they do not think for themselves and are slaves to the opinion of others. Dr. Waldo Vieira, wrote, and I agree, "So many of us follow what we were told to do." One of the programming patterns was to behave. "Behave" meant to control—and control is stopping the flow. Therefore, do yourself a big favor: learn from your emotions instead of hiding and avoiding them, in order to be healthier, more loving, wealthier, and caring.

"Eventually we must realize that Emotions are as important as life itself."

To understand a little bit better about the importance of emotional release, we must go back in time to our childhood, to find out how our feelings began to take shape and what caused us to get in touch with them. It's very important to recognize incidents from the past, whether it was one or various family members who hurt us, or incidents in school, or with our best friend, or anything that made us feel, insecure, scared, hurt or angry.

Emotional traumas help us to go deep into our insecurities and fear, to overcome, learn about them, get stronger and release them. They also help us to mature and grow spiritually. I always say, "There is no warrior without war." Unfortunately, or fortunately, the harder the road, the better the lesson—particularly for the stubborn ones like myself.

When we are young we don't know how to deal with our emotions very well. The people who had any influence in our lives programmed our minds one way or the other, telling us what to do and how to do it. In addition, if school friends make fun of us, scare us or call us names, we think, at that age, that something is wrong with us; we believe in what they said. Our minds have the ability to store everything we experience in early age, putting some of the unpleasant things in the little box called the subconscious mind.

Once we deliver that unpleasant information to the subconscious, we have the impression, on the conscious level that the unpleasant feeling is no longer there. We fool ourselves, thinking that avoiding the subject, not dealing with the emotions, saves us from the pain the particular incident caused.

How many times have we very quickly said, 'I DON'T WANT TO TALK ABOUT IT!' when someone begins talking about something that targets our pain? That's the same as saying, 'I DON'T WANT TO DEAL WITH MY EMOTION!" This goes on for the rest of our lives if we don't stop and treat it with the same care we treat any disease we experience. The medicine for the blockage is to acknowledge emotion and release it.

To meet our evolutionary goals, we must know about emotion—respect it, feel it, and release it, whenever necessary. Just as when we're hungry we eat, and when feeling sleepy, we go to sleep.

10

THE GATEWAY OF EMOTIONAL ENERGIES

Chakras are our energetic centers, and are, therefore, the emotional centers as well. They are the transducers of universal energy. Because there is a biochemical residual in the cells, they pick up all the many frequencies out there. When the flow of this process is blocked, retarded, or obstructed by trauma, memories, chronic pain, attitudes, beliefs or the intellectual self, anything that triggers cellular memory will stimulate the original trauma.

Remember that the chakras are the intermediaries between the two bodies and are the channels responsible for the processing of energetic emotional charges, the "focal point, gateway, or the way in and out." There are seven most commonly known chakras and others, such as those on the palms of our hands and bottom of our feet:

First—The Root Center, based on the spine (corresponds to survival, life source)

Second—The Sexual Center, beneath the navel (corresponding to self-esteem, sexual attachment, jealousy, abandonment)

Third—The Fear Center, in the solar plexus/diaphragm (self control, control of others, submission, power)

Fourth—The Heart Center, in the area of the heart (sympathetic and empathetic emotions, pain, compassion, soul memory)

Fifth—The Throat Center, at the throat level (corresponds to communication, creativity, trust, self-expression)

Sixth—The Coronary Center, is the third eye (inner vision, ability to see and intuitive phenomena)

Seventh—The Crown Center, in the middle of top of the head (unemotional, connection to the source, enlightenment state)

11

THE ROLE OF EMOTIONS IN THE FOUR LEVELS OF HEALING

As we mentioned at the beginning of this book, the human life consists of four aspects: the spiritual, mental, emotional and physical levels of existence. Only when we mature and heal these four levels, do we have a chance to fulfill our lives in balance, wholeness and happiness.

Most of humanity is familiar with the spiritual level—religion, beliefs, meditation, etc; the mental level—our intellect and knowledge; and the physical level—our physical body, health, disease, fitness, etc. When we talk about emotions, we realize that people have the tendency to hide them, for the simple reason that they represent the unknown. For example, sometimes we "lose control" of a situation and get caught up in an argument with someone. Our heart begins to beat faster, our blood gets really hot, and our voice gets louder and louder, and we are not able to control it. As a consequence, some of us avoid any kind of arguments, because we think that anger is destructive and negative. On the other hand, we can face that anger and analyze why that particular emotion visited us and what triggered the feeling.

Mental level

The different levels of the subconscious mind not only influence physical body functions, but they give us access to the consciousness of other dimensions as well. They integrate our emotional, mental, and spiritual states into physical expression. This is why in holistic healing, the healer always looks for the metaphysical cause behind a physical problem.

Learning to work with the mind and affect it from all levels—physical, emotional, mental, and spiritual—is the key to establish balanced health.

Studying and analyzing a situation helps our feelings to be acknowledged, and opens the way for their job to be done. Our body reacts with electricity and sends that electricity to our energetic field when we feel. Afterwards, we should speak to the person involved using our analytical mind, making an effort to show them that we're thinking on both sides of the situation. It's okay to be angry with someone, even if that someone is your own mother or father. The guilt accompanying this feeling of anger is a tremendous setback in our existential process.

Another example is the feeling of love. Most of us, when we're in love, feel as if we are in a dream state most of the time; smiling at everyone, nervous when we see or don't see our mates, saying and doing things we thought we never would.

EMOTIONS ARE VERY POWERFUL TOOLS FOR THE RELEASE OF ENERGY.

The fact that we control our feelings for our own reasons builds energetic resistance to our body's nature. We block the flux of life force we should normally experience and this will promote disease in the body. This resistance becomes another feeling—the fear of feeling deeply.

As you see WE CANNOT GET AWAY FROM FEELINGS! We can fool ourselves, acting like we are the coolest beings in the universe, but deep inside, we know better. Besides, blocking the emotions, as with any other energy force, blocks life itself. As the blood flows in our veins, energy needs to be free, doing what it's supposed to be doing.

When we have an infection, it means that our blood was blocked in that spot; pain escalates until we can't take it anymore. Blocked emotions cause us to go through a similar process regarding sadness, depression, headaches, etc. To refine the energy and help it to takes its course, helps us feel better, to feel proud of our actions, to feel relief.

Also, taking actions against our own emotional blockages helps others at the same time. How many times have we ended a good friendship or a relationship because of a lack of communication? That means we couldn't handle the situation when anger or sadness took over. No matter what, it's important to acknowledge our feelings to ourselves and to others, so they and we can have the opportunity to learn from them.

12

SEEKING LOVE

We all want to be loved by someone, whether it's our mother, father or friend. Because we are energetic beings and love is part of us, it completes us, satisfying our deepest needs for togetherness (which affects our physical health) and being understood and appreciated (affecting our psychological well-being).

When we are babies we love hugs, kisses and attention. Nothing changes; we just act like we don't care as much in adulthood, because of defense mechanisms such as fear of rejection, embarrassment, etc. But the truth is that we are all suckers for good affection.

The two essential principles of life are expressed in eastern philosophy as yin (male) and yang (female) energies. We all carry these two principals within ourselves and as we bring the feminine and masculine principles into balance, we create harmony, and therefore health, within.

Relationship is one of the most powerful paths that exists. It's a great tool to teach us about ourselves, if we know how to learn from it. Our partners are powerful teachers. We are seeking to become whole, so we are attracted to people who carry the energies that are undeveloped in our own personalities.

Our sexuality is also related to the flow of energetic life force we carry. It's connected deeply with our needs for touch, affection, pleasure, acceptance, sharing and togetherness.

We grow up in an environment of difficulties of all sorts, but that is exactly why we are here, to learn lessons as a result of these difficulties. Emotions serve to protect us when we fear a situation or person; to signal we are in love with someone, to stop someone from taking advantage of us; to send the signal of sadness when something is not right, and in many other ways.

As a consequence of our control patterns, some things happen in our lives over and over again, for example, when a woman or man is always in love with someone that rejects her or him. They keep complaining about the situation (or they don't complain at all, and just put up with it). They know they deserve better, but in reality, they get attracted to the same type of person over and over again.

This type of behavior originates in childhood, when they were rejected by someone they loved deeply and were mistreated by that person. As a result, the child's brain registers that this was what they deserved, and they perceive themselves, throughout their lives, as being attracted to their own image (mirror); someone who will understand, and remind them of, their pain.

In most cases, this kind of relationship falls apart. The pain remains there and never goes away, because two people who have the same blockage are looking for change, and they will try to change their partner in order to feel wanted. Their partner is seeking the same result, and their efforts become a two-way street. One constantly trying to change the other generates conflict and arguments.

Another example is someone like myself; someone who was poor throughout most of their childhood and someone they admired and trusted, tells them, 'This is what life is about—and that's that!' The child accepts this as truth. Normally, this kind of person works very hard to achieve financial success, but can't make it through the way they would like to. The reasons may vary due to the many levels of emotion the child had to struggle through; low self-esteem or guilt could be a factor.

Only when we grow out of this cycle, break the chains from the past, and realize that we must change ourselves, and not the other person, are we on our way to self-love and self-healing. That is when we start to see life in a different light; we begin to be more selective with our friendships and relationships. We start working toward a better place and more self-value. We speak out more; we no longer get bent out of shape with fear of talking to our boss about a raise, and no longer fear being alone. We begin to realize that we can, and must, know ourselves better, that it's okay to be with ourselves, at least for a while, in order to organize our ideas and analyze our lives in a different light.

It is easier to change ourselves than to keep trying to change another person.

Our main lesson in life is to LOVE OURSELVES. Everything else is a result of that lesson. Think about it: we study in order to better learn how to survive, we work to live better. We get married to be loved better; we have children as a result of love. Everything we do, no matter what, is a result of self-satisfaction, the need for survival, the love of self and the love of others.

Starting the change with "self" is fundamental. It is a process, a continuing process of renewal, based on the belief system of each person.

When we have dependent self, we expect relationships to fill the needs we are unable to fill for ourselves.

When we have balanced self, we expect relationships to enhance us as individuals, while taking full responsibility for ourselves.

The truth is, we are born alone. We must grow up and learn how to do things on our own such as; shower, eat, read, etc...the same goes for success and achievement.

Loving someone will be beneficial to us when we fully understand the principal of unconditional love for ourselves. In my point of view, we cannot give what we do not have, nor relate in a positive way to another person if we don't truly know what unconditional love is about. We can achieve self-love with self determination, patience, awareness, knowledge and focus, as well as lots of concentration, motivation and meditation.

The human life consists of four aspects: the spiritual, mental, emotional and physical levels of existence. Only when we mature and heal these four levels, do we have a chance to fulfill our lives in balance, wholeness and happiness.

Healing methods such as yoga, massage, acupuncture and exercises, are great tools for the healing process on the physical level. But only when we use healing for the four levels do we get to the genuine freedom. Reiki, for example, is very good on the spiritual level. Knowledge is wonderful food for the mental level and Alternative Emotional Release techniques using physical touch, energy and spiritual guidance help make the connection between the different levels of healing.

Again, healing begins with self-love. *Self—love is the most important relationship in our lives; it's the foundation of all other relationships.* When that relationship works, then all the other relationships will work as well. When we focus on that inner relationship, we will be able to see everything else reflecting what we feel inside. Through this process we will create more truthful and fulfilling relationships with others.

13

THERE ARE NO NEGATIVE EMOTIONS!

There are no negative emotions! We act negatively as a result of chronic emotional pain.

I can't begin to tell you how many times I've heard and read the term, "negative emotions" from doctors, speakers, teacher and all kinds of people everywhere. Every time I hear this my reaction is the same: I want to have a voice and show the world that our emotions are not negative whatsoever; they are a result of past unhealthy experiences. So please! Don't blame negative actions on the emotions! Their only duty is to guide us to resolve the past issues we came here to learn from.

Emotions will help us to understand better what is going on with us, in relation to everything. We cannot afford to ignore our emotions without punishment as a result. The traumas, fears, sadness and phobias will remain in our subconscious minds until the day we decide to face them fully and then release them, for good. When we release the old feeling from our subconscious and consequently, our physical body, we have a sense of lightness and the freedom to experience other situations and to expand our horizons much further. We start to see things we didn't see before and feel differently about others and ourselves, as if there is another life to be lived from then on.

I can't put in words the exact feeling of freedom we experience when we release emotional blockages, because feelings cannot be explained one hundred percent with words, only with actions. The only way one knows what others are feeling is to feel the same. Only then will we be able to truly understand.

Emotions are very powerful energetic experiences. They must be taken care of, in order to protect us properly, instead of harming us.

When we feel emotional about something, we should acknowledge and express it, without trying to go against it, because that is what makes us go wild, crazy and become uncontrolled, eventually. Thinking about it with care and maturity makes us realize that particular feeling is there for a reason, and that reason needs to be acknowledged as well, in a reasonable manner, and than released, without losing control. Even if you do lose control, acknowledge that as well. Tell the person you're arguing with that their action is making you really mad. Results can come in many different ways; we must be creative with our actions in a way that teaches ourselves as well as others. Don't forget, however, that whoever comes in touch with us in this lifetime comes for a reason. We must deal with them one way or the other, so we having nothing to lose in doing the best we can and learning from that situation.

We can choose to see every person's attitude as a learning process. That way, we gain from the situation, instead of seeing it as something that is negative or is trying to destroy us. Don't forget that the other person also has gone through problems and pain; that's why she or he can look so obnoxious to us sometimes. Their insecurities lead them to aggressiveness and rudeness. Being aware of the reasons behind the action that causes people to touch us on such a deep level helps us to understand. Seeing others in a positive light will help us to grow. I know it's a very difficult lesson to learn, but it's not impossible if you are seeking other levels of knowledge and experiences on earth. If you really meet this challenge, you will feel like you are above all the negativity that people normally get caught up in. These blockages stop their flow of light, happiness, love and health. But we will know better and life will become easier to manage altogether.

A good way to live life better is to view it optimistically. The more fun you have, the better. See sometimes how funny situations can be, taking us to a higher level of existence. That is what makes talented comedians—seeing life's routines on a different level. Routine becomes hard to handle when we see it as seriously as most people do. There are always two sides of the coin: the positive and the negative, night and day, black and white, happy and sad, and so on.

If we choose to see life pessimistically, we will; if we decide to see life optimistically, we will. For example, if someone is rude to you, anywhere or for whatever reason, and while smiling, you tell them so, chances are that person will react more positively than otherwise. If the person persists, that means she or he is not ready to deal with positive reaction. Then you do whatever comes to mind to alleviate the situation in a clever way. Be creative. Show that person that you are on a positive level. Let them learn from your positive attitude instead of you playing their negative game. I know that reacting positively to a negative situation is very hard, but that is exactly what life puts on the plate for us to learn—how to resolve difficulties with maturity. Just keep on exercising your will and don't give up on your lessons. It will pay off eventually. I guarantee it!

Let's not forget that other peoples' struggles can be much worse than ours. Let's honor the presence of others on our path and treat them with respect as a healing medicine of love and understanding, instead of what they are used to.

The natural order for human expression is: see or hear something, react to it with feeling, think it over, and words will be expressed. Words are powerful tools. They are the natural way of expressing ourselves. If we don't pay attention to this natural process, we end up saying things we don't mean and eventually hurt the situation instead of fixing it. Many times I could hit myself for not having seen a difficult situation involving others in a more relaxed manner, despite my efforts. But I kept working on it. I still have places to go on that level, but today I am expressing my feelings in the most impeccable way possible for my own emotional health. I am aware of my limitations and I acknowledge them with honor.

The way we bring information into our minds and senses (audio, visual and feeling) is through good communication. If we don't communicate our message to others, we won't be able to survive in this world in a positive manner.

Normally, we like people who like us, so it's a good habit to like people, in order to be liked. If you have a problem with this philosophy, you must have some anger against people for some reason. That needs to be taken care of with emotional release treatment.

I have found the words of Stephen R. Covey in his book, "The 7 Habits of Highly Effective People," to be critical to our effectiveness in terms of communication.

"Communication is the most important skill in life. We spend most of our waking hours communicating. But consider this: You've spent years learning how to read and write, years learning how to speak. But what about listening? What training or education have you had that enables you to listen so that you really, deeply understand another human being from that individual's own frame of reference?

"We typically seek first to be understood. Most people do not listen with the intent to understand; they listen with the intent to reply. They're either speaking or preparing to speak. They're filtering everything through their own paradigms, reading their autobiography into other people's lives!"

14

MOST DISEASES ARE CAUSED BY EMOTIONAL BLOCKAGES IN THIS OR OTHER LIFETIMES

Most physical diseases are a result of emotional blockages. There is a saying; "We are what we eat." No doubt about that, but isn't what we eat a result of how we feel? Think about it. How many times because of sadness or depression, do we eat whatever is in the refrigerator? Or, even though we know that sugar and chocolate are bad for us, we still eat them, particularly if we are depressed? I realize that poor people eat more, in quantity, than wealthy people. Everything that would give us more pleasure, we become addicted to, in order to avoid depression or unwanted thoughts.

The cause of all emotional problems is a disruption in the body's energy system.

There are a variety of cases in clinical medicine with emotional roots of which clinical physicians are not aware. Yet, there are millions of people discovering the power of alternative medicine for a very simple reason—it works. If the traditional treatments take too long, be aware that might be a sign that you should look for healing elsewhere. I am not implying that clinical doctors are bad guys. There are many clinical doctors who mean well and are very devoted to their profession. But in the majority of clinical cases, doctors fail to look for the real roots of a physical condition. The medicine subscribed will treat just one level of the patient's problem. This is why psychology patients go to numerous sessions without sufficient, deep results right away, if at all. The clinical psychological method operates on the conscious level, and the analytical mind has been sabotaging our happiness for years—why should it be different in a doctor's office?

When healing by energetic means, there is no outside remedy. The problem is solved by our own mind, which produces the blockage to dissolve, naturally allowing our life force to flow freely. Emotions give us the ability to experience life deeply in relation to other beings and the world. That is why the emotions hold such importance in our existence.

When we feel like reacting to any action by others, and are forced to control that reaction, we keep that frustrated feeling blocked inside of our subconscious for the rest of our lives.

A good example of the physical results of emotional blockages, is common lower back pain. Back pain is as mystifying today as it was decades ago. Despite excellent tests and procedures, modern back specialists admit that up to 80% of all cases have "no clear physiologic causes." In fact, many pain-free people show aggravated disease in X-rays. Back specialists focus primarily on patients who have jobs involving heavy and frequent lifting or prolonged standing or sitting. These working conditions do have an important influence on our physical bodies, but the combination of mental and emotional stress on the job is what forces our nerve systems to malfunction. As the nerve system is directly connected to our spine, the energetic charge goes straight to our back, forcing it to malfunction.

I had seven years of lower back pain. Once I discovered that it was all emotional stress for lack of security and self-esteem, I started to work on exercising my mind to trust the positive forces of the universe. I became a much better individual and kind to myself. It was either that, or die.

Another example is chronic fatigue syndrome. Prolonged fatigue can be a symptom of a number of conditions, including anemia, depression, chronic infection, candida, auto-immune disorder and cancer. For the majority of cases of extreme fatigue, no apparent cause can be found, even though the problem may persist. Although some doctors still dismiss it as all in the mind, it is recognized as a debilitating and very real condition.

As we are energetic beings, let's be aware of the importance of energy and work on the nuances and various levels of healing, in order to learn how to be completely happy. Yes, it is possible to be completely happy if one sees life positively. Once we're healed, there is no stopping. We feel as if the power of our self-love is going to help us to transcend time, space and old wounds.

A good exercise to check on our patterns is to ask:

—Am I satisfied with everything in my life right now?
—What in my life could be improved?
—How can I approach self-improvement?

Do whatever attracts you. Look for things that you always desired, but never had the opportunity, to do. Or find new things that would take you to other levels of excitement.

The energy force that moves us is the force of all things in the universe, which can't be truly explained by scientists, or by anyone else, for that matter. When we seek an explanation using words, limitation and frustration take over.

The energy force that gives us life is to be felt, experienced, respected and acknowledged by all living things.

Emotional unhealthy states:

AFRAID	HURT	POWERLESS	ANGRY
Appalled	Afflicted	Disbelieving	Annoyed
Awkward	Agonized	Depressed	Bitter
Cowardly	Crushed	Exhausted	Enraged
Dismayed	Distressed	Frustrated	Indignant
Doubtful	Despairing	Guilty	Infuriated
Lonely	Injured	Isolated	Irritated
Panicked	Sad	Numb	Offended
Restless	Suffering	Regretful	Resentful
Shaky	Tortured	Shamed	Etc...

All the states above carry a lesson to be learned from past experiences. Healing will only take place if our interpretation of that feeling is observed and resolved within us.

15

EMOTIONAL DUTY

We are here to evolve and to learn how to live in harmony within ourselves, with others and with the environment. That is our challenge in this dimension. One way or the other, we will have to get there, even if we keep coming back many lifetimes. It's like in school, when we don't pass the test and have to repeat the grade until we get it right. To be honest within ourselves and with others is a must. Maintaining positive thoughts help us to cope with our journey, and also takes us to a higher level energetically.

When we evolve, we feel the urge to help others as well. Feeling love, joy and happiness inside inspires us to share. We give everything we have inside, including anger and depression. How many times have you noticed a group of people exchanging happiness, when all of a sudden, an individual arrives and the energy of the group immediately changes, and nobody quite understands why? The energy that emanates from an individual will irradiate or contaminate all around, in seconds.

Our energy is what guides us, attracts us and charges us. It's impossible to get away from it. Don't even think about it—you're just retarding an inevitable learning process. Time is relative, because it's seems to be the same in all dimensions. That's why we have deja vu or feel like we have seen or met people, or have been certain places, before.

Maybe a good way to check, so to speak, on your performance as a person, is to write down on paper, duties to accomplish in order to achieve your goals. I will give you an example. There are many things to accomplish in this lifetime, but I will focus on three at this time.

—Judging ourselves or judging others. (We have to work very hard on this one.) We will begin to focus where we are supposed to. We get distracted from the real lesson if we waste our time and attention on the higher purpose of our encounters and situations.

—Dependency on others. Most of us grow up to believe that someone else should take care of us or that is someone else's fault what happens to us, and so on…But, let's face it! We were born alone! Dependent people need others to get what they want. Unless we are paralyzed or disabled we should not need this.

—Dependency on material things. Attachment to money, clothes, objects etc. So many of us become extremely attached to material things; sometimes people prefer to die than live without their objects and money. Many people die every day during robberies, just because they reacted to protect their assets. The workplace is filled with people who live in emotional turmoil, hating their job or their bosses, but continuing to spend their time and money on material things, Balanced spending is okay; I'm referring to the massive numbers of people who are constantly seeking the momentary pleasure: the act of buying, forgetting about the day after. Watch out for this pattern, it's very popular and powerful.

16

OUR EVOLUTION & EMOTIONS

o o o o o o o o o o o o o o o o o o o o o o o o o o o o o o o

"To evolve is to completely domesticate and to employ energy with greater intelligence."

—Waldo Vieira

To aid in understanding a little about this complex process of evolution, I will simplify here, some information on the subject. It's important for all of us to know more about our existence from a broad view.

It is said that we choose to be born in the physical body again, in order to learn more and to have additional experiences in order to help our evolutionary process. It is also said that we know exactly which parents we'd like to have once we take over the physical body.

There are various dimensions and we exist in all of them at the same time. If this is too complicated to understand, just ease into it, using dreams as an example. In dreams, we experience all the sensations of this dimension, but we are in an altered state of mind. That is why we can easily fly and do other things in the dreamtime without fear. We may also become terrified when dreaming of danger and know inside that we must wake up in order to stop the process.

Another body that is very important for our evolution is the holochakra, where our chakras act as intermediaries between the bodies. It's also the channel responsible for energetic emotional charges. Again, the literal translation of "chakra" is the "focal point, gateway, the way in and out." It's in the chakras that the memory of old energy is saved. It goes to the "recycle box" until we decide to delete it. The chakras keep the information intact until we revise it and fix it the way we want it to be. Only we have the power to take action to fix it or change it. Good healers will guide you through this process; look for them; they are around. Use their touch in order to make your life better.

Finally, our soul or psychosoma, is in touch with, and is being watched by, "helpers." I perceive these as what many people call "angels." Obviously, there are other dimensions and therefore, other beings in those dimensions communicating to us all the time, but the majority of us don't pay much attention. It is also important to mention here that we all have the capacity to communicate with beings from other dimensions. Or, we can say that we all have psychic abilities, we simply are not knowledgeable on the subject, and, therefore, we don't practice enough to become good at it.

To evolve, we must think for ourselves and believe in ourselves. How can we do it if we are not assured of our opinions and beliefs? Billions of people are slaves, manipulated by their leaders, whether these leaders are family members, schoolteachers, politicians or religious leaders. Part of the evolving process is to believe in ourselves. Be creative and create your own reality, finding your mission on earth, helping others and yourself. The balance of a person's life depends on what the person thinks, feels, and does.

Human life has never reached as advanced a level of evolution as it has today. Many of us are running to alternative methods of healing, instead of the old clinical methods, because we are waking up. We are in the process of regaining our power that was lost thousands of years ago in powerful centers of knowledge such as Atlantis. In order to evolve, we must to learn to deal with emotions in a more comprehensive and rational way. The only way this is possible is to learn from the old traumas, cleansing ourselves of the old (past lives as well as this lifetime) for the sake of present and future emotional experiences.

*Our evolutionary process has progressed over thousands of years. Life after life, we accumulate innumerous experiences and knowledge that results in our present state. If we are truly the result of what we construct in our evolutionary progression, which is conquered step by-step, let us work towards engendering a more agile and aware rhythm in our evolution.

For everything there is a process
For everyone there is a lesson
Even if we are aged
Never is it too late to learn that patience
is a great exercise for evolution

In the tolerance of knowledge
In the calmness of leisure
In the understanding of life
And in the consciousness of the force behind power

*This statement is based on the consciousness research of the International Institute of Projectiology and Conscientiology, of which I am a member. The classes are touched with the commitment of many volunteers to pass on this important message to us so that we may become more aware on the conscious level of each and every one of us. If you feel inclined to learn more details about our evolution you can go to the IIPC web: **www.iipc.org**

17

EMOTIONS & SEX

Sex and Emotions are the most sensitive subjects to talk about in human life. Emotion, for its sensitive nature, and sex, for the discrimination it attracts.

One of the reasons Sex is the most moneymaking of all businesses is that the majority of people, particularly men, confuse sex with emotional affection. The touch of the physical body is what these people translate as affection.

Our sexuality is related to the flow of energy, of life force. Because we are made out of energy, sex is a tremendous energetic drive as well. It is deeply connected with our emotions. The more we open our minds and express our emotions, the better we will relate ourselves to sex and the pleasures of the life force.

The prejudice against sex by religion, society and schools is the main force behind all the sexually abusive behaviors of sick minds.

We must be honest with ourselves in order to even begin to deal with a partner in a sexual relationship that will be authentic and mature. The fear of rejection, the insecurities about physical body limitations, fear of being judged by the partner and other concerns, come from old experiences carried in our subconscious mind and transferred to our most private time with a partner. Only after a period of self-knowledge can we overcome traumas and the belief system of others. Only then, can we feel totally free sexually, with a partner.

The courage to talk and communicate to our partner ALL our fantasies, limitations, and whatever else we it feel necessary to share, is a tremendous help to the partners in the sexual relationship. It is harder for some than others, but is by all means necessary, for a more rewarding performance on both ends.

The honesty, courage and creativity will come with the release of old emotional blockages and unpleasant experiences will free one's mind and soul to start fresh regarding everything in life, including sex.

When we free the old unwanted patterns, we begin to love ourselves, and therefore accept ourselves with all the "stuff" we believed stopped us before. That is when we open our throat chakra for communication purposes. The more we talk about our struggles and fantasies, and the greater our interest in knowing them, the greater are our chances of gaining our partner's confidence. On the other hand, this also helps our partner to feel free enough to open up with us. This mutual trust will enliven the sexual confidence necessary for a lifetime achievement regarding sex.

Because in childhood many of us were told that sex was dirty and nasty, we believed it. To break with that belief, we have to practice as much as we can our communication skills with our partner. We should not forget that we are intelligent beings, but we are also animals by instinct. We know how to survive in our physical realm.

Many of us feel so ashamed of our own sexuality that we deny a great deal of this incredible energetic potential. Because of our denials, our society has become obsessed with physical sexuality. Because of sexual extremes and controlling measures by society, distorted sexual actions such as sexual abuse take place.

Sex is physical, emotional, and mental, as well as spiritual. On the physical level, sex satisfies our physical body; on the emotional level, it satisfies our feelings of togetherness. On the mental level, we're satisfied by the fantasy and the vast creative possibilities our minds produce, with various positions, setups and discovery. Finally, there is the deep spiritual connection we can feel to another person, including those from other lives or dimensional experiences with whom we have unfinished business and duties. A lot of us practice on one of the levels or even two or three, and are satisfied by that. But to feel a complete sexual experience, we must go for the four levels at once.

"Sex is extremely important for everyone's life without exception." We owe it to ourselves to release our sexual energy, as a matter of respect for all natural phenomena, all facets of ourselves as energetic beings. It is part of the entire energetic cycle. Those who think this is unimportant, are probably controlling their life force and in denial of their own instincts because of traumatic experiences with family in the past or because of religious beliefs. Some religions demand total abstinence and some religious practitioners either release their sexual energy while hiding from others, feeling guilty in the process, or have to take medicine to stop this powerful energetic connection with their own bodies.

18

FINANCIAL SUCCESS AND EMOTIONS

"Is There Any Relation between Financial Success and Our Emotions?"

MONEY!—The incredible "symbol" that just about 99% of humans focus on gaining for survival.

We can choose to have money as our servant instead as our master. We can make money working in a 9 to 5 setting, where everything is dictated for us and "security" comes in the form of a salary with benefits. Or we can find confidence enough to use our minds to "create" our own survival strategies and fulfill ourselves in this lifetime.

On the first side of the coin, is what the large majority of people rely on, because that was what the majority of us were programmed to believe by our peers and family. We were told that we should do, or be, this and that, according to others' standards and their evaluation of their own experiences. They believed that the only way to get security was to work for the system, where everything is already set up for them. It is very common to see a new generation believing in what the older generation believed. The way our minds were developed, the old way may appear easier, because people don't have to think in terms of the big picture. All they have to do is show up every day (in most cases), do their specific duty, be on time, and get the check at the end of the pay period.

In general, this idea is a continuation of the parental input into the individual's belief system and it makes them feel comfortable to have a means of survival for their own good and for the good of their families. According to their life plan, everything goes well with the retirement plan, vacations, car, house, etc...So after awhile, one maybe feels they have done their job. At a certain age they will be ready to retire, rest, or finally take the vacation they dreamed about. Perhaps then, they will await death comfortably, and not care that life was not adventurous, after all.

On the other side of the coin, it's a matter of self-confidence. This road is a warrior's choice. One has to go against a lot of criticism and obstacles in order to survive despite what "they" believe. The warrior kind is one who confronts the opposition of society every day. Sometimes, when the pressure gets too tough, they must go back and forth into their belief systems, but the warrior kind never gives up, continuing on their chosen road to the accomplishment of their vision. It is never easy for the warrior kind, since, in the majority of cases, there is tremendous pressure regarding money, investment of time, financing, education, guidance, etc.

When I say "warrior" I mean the ones who find, inside of themselves, the reason for their coming and staying in this existence; Those who look inside to find their MISSION on earth and then help others on their journeys to see the light of evolution. These are the ones who understand the need to find the essence of their vital life purpose.

So many of us come and go without even touching the subject of our life purpose. It is imperative that more of us spread the message and set examples for a better existence on this planet, because after all, what we do and believe will be for the good of all of us, as we are one part of a "big whole. It's like a big community; whatever we do affects people around us, whether we notice or not; whether we want it to or not. So if we are powerful, we will project power around us. We are always observing and curious about success, and we want to be successful as well.

The concept of "We are one" comes from the fact that we are ALL made of the same energy field and cells, and, therefore, power. We are all powerful. It is just a matter of recognizing it, cleansing it and utilizing it, like everything else in our lives.

Each one of us has a mission on this journey and it's up to us to find out what we are here for and how are we going to accomplish our goal according to "the plan." Accomplishing the plan of life is what will lead us to our happiness and fulfillment, as well as to our freedom.

One of the warriors I met in this existence told me: "I will work with a particular institution, selling or donating the fine work I have done through the years, and that is fine. But what I will not do, is sell myself, or allow them to own me."

Regarding self-assurance and confidence, it is necessary to work on our emotions. Emotional blockages will not allow the true selves to come out and be free. There are many alternative healing modalities that can be used for this purpose. I suggest that everyone reading this article who feels they have an emotional issue, (99.9% of us do) research and find for themselves the emotional solutions that satisfy their quest for personal freedom. Then shoot for the stars!

Once we are free from that old baggage and outdated emotional turmoil, we are finally free to experience our utmost essence of Self on earth, in all dimensions. Emotions are what lead us to want to do things or not—period. It's about time for humanity to realize that just about everything we do is because of an emotional signal.

Whenever we feel the urge, we must seek as much information on the subject as possible, finding the one or more healing modalities that attract us and feel right for us to work on.

Time is money, the financial people say, so to be successful on all levels, (spiritual, mental, physical and emotional) one must be aware of the work entailed that has to be done in ALL areas, in order to grasp the meaning of existence.

If the most financially successful people in the world don't have their emotions taken care of, they will not, and cannot, manage to be truly happy and fulfilled.

"MONEY HAS NO POWER, YOU DO."

"Money is nothing but a symbol made with paper and metal, created by us, and for us, to exchange for material things to possess." Cut the drama—money is not an impossible giant, one that only a few can, or have, the knowledge, to touch. We ALL have enough willpower to program to win the battle of survival and abundance. It requires focus, less laziness, more motivation and self-confidence. It is an investment of our attention and respect, like any other business in life.

For the warriors to get financially successful, we must know what our mission or plan is, in order to inspire us to create the right product, message, or way to help others. Helping others honestly will activate the recycling process, and the inevitable feedback will take place, like a snowball. In short, people will look for you for what you have to offer to society. That is all, folks. It's that simple. If we can create and materialize situations around us, we certainly can create and materialize money around us, as well. Life is a game and money is the card that brings material comfort. It is not the most important thing like a lot of people think. The most important thing is YOU and how to learn to accomplish survival, using your intelligence and creativity to help others to do the same. If you don't know the rules, you cannot win. Know that you can start practicing until you get so good at it that you will be smart enough to create your own strategy to get to victory.

Sometimes we tell ourselves that we don't want to deal with the boring financial stuff. I used to say to myself; 'I don't know anything about that stuff and I don't want to know! It gives me a headache!' Instead of learning about money and taking charge, I would give it to my boyfriend at the time to deal with for me.

KNOW about money. Read everything about it. Get a financial adviser. When I decided to learn about money I made an appointment with a good financial consultant for help with my plan for abundance and to share smart strategies to getting there in my planned period. If you want to know of a good financial adviser who will help you for free, give me a call and we will recommend one to you. If we choose to have money in our lives we cannot afford to be afraid of it, we must relate to it in a positive manner. Get to know how to save, invest and attract.

Life gives magnificent, unlimited opportunities to learn. The challenge is that those opportunities are disguised as difficult problems to solve. Our duty is to focus on the solutions, and not on the problem itself. That way, life becomes a game to play with joy, instead of in desperation.

Getting to genuine freedom and happiness is hard for some, but not impossible, and once we get there—"Holy cow!" It feels…WOW! No words can describe, or even explain, the feeling! The only way to understand this feeling is to FEEL it. So remember…

If we don't free our emotions, we won't be free.
If we don't get free, we won't be happy.
If we don't get happy, we won't be healthy.
If we don't get healthy, we will die.

If we die like this, we will have to come back to learn what we didn't learn this time.

So, we might as well learn at once, and stop going around in existential circles.

19

EMOTIONS & RELIGION

Religion is a good thing to use as a tool for focusing attention, organization, discipline, social life, etc., particularly at a young age, when we haven't yet developed attributes. Most religions have the hierarchic structure of a leader followed by associates or helpers. In this structure, one is supposed to follow the leader: his or her beliefs cannot be questioned or doubted. There is also the community setting, where a group of people lead certain communities and the general community must follow the rules created by the top group. In both cases, there is a common scenario: one must follow the rules.

One will follow other people's beliefs and actions easier, because our minds have been programmed to follow our parents, our schoolteachers, etc. This method is well received by the majority of humans, because of the structure of our childhood. It is also easier to follow the crowd. When we decide to question our life existence, asking things such as: 'Where do we come from? What are we doing here? What is our mission/plan on this planet?'—we begin to move way from the leadership setting, and start to follow our own minds and beliefs. We begin to see, feel, or hear, instinctual signals about our own truth. In other words, we grasp our unique plan of action, what we came here to do—taking responsibility for everything we learn and providing guidance to help in the evolution of other humans.

When we begin the process of evolution, we come to believe in ourselves more and more, to the point of self-sufficiency. In other words, believing and trusting in our own belief systems, instead of following others. This process guides us to create our own world according to our level of awareness.

History tells us this phenomenon has been repeated, over and over, through time. The vast majority of people follow opinions without even questioning whether the majority is right or not. People assume that if the majority came to that conclusion, then it must be right. Let's use the example of Jesus being tortured by the same people he helped. Those people believed that what they were doing was the right thing, because the large majority, together with their leader, said so. The crowd had fears and insecurities about Jesus. He saw their limitations and insecurities, and so, forgave them. His growth process serves until today, as an example of maturity and evolution.

It is hard to forgive people who hurt us, but if we look at their actions as part of the learning process, we are going to get smarter with each lesson, and forgive them as well. When an action by another person hurts us, we must look for the roots of that pain. If we look at it from an analytical point of view, we will see the person's problems, stemming from the past, which led to the action in the present.

Most of us hurt each other because of our own limitations and fear/insecurities. And if we are limited in our growth, we are acting like kids in the evolutionary process. If a child slaps us in the face, instead of hitting the child back, we advise that child, or firmly tell the child why that should not happen again, (because we "know" the child doesn't know better). The same thing goes for adults, particularly those who are ignorant (don't know better) on the subject of emotions and evolution. There is a lesson for them to learn from us, and vice versa. The more we guide people to the light, the more light we are going to have for ourselves on our existential journey.

Life gives us magnificent, unlimited opportunities to learn. The challenge is that those opportunities are disguised as difficult problems to solve. Our duty is to focus on the solutions, and not on the problem itself. That way, life becomes a game to play with joy, instead of in desperation.

I suggest that we all create our own religion regarding our own belief system. Since people just like us created religions, why can't we create our own?

Most religions preach: 'Be good to others, support the congregation, socialize, pray/meditate, etc.' Well, we can do all that also, when we create our own religion. Practice in your own place, inside of your house, with your neighbors, in your work setting, with your family.

Don't wait for a holiday to hug your friends or to talk about important things in life, such as old traumas and issues. Practice your own religion in the subways and on the streets. Be positive and motivated with the love that you have inside. Because you invested and have succeeded, now you are a millionaire regarding love. This is when we can afford to give emotional donations to our friends and people who cross our paths to be helped and guided by us, and vice-versa.

Comparing Jesus' teaching with what I am conveying here, provides the core meaning of this message. Maybe the new, massive consciousness is what is going to change the world and peoples' misery. Love for the self is the answer. Only if we have love inside, will we be able to share it outside correctly.

20

RECIPE FOR CREATION OF A BETTER LIFE

Some of us think we have to be extra special in order to be creative. We can be creative with everything around us: our jobs, kids, the way we handle the rudeness of others on the subway or during rush-hour traffic, or just dealing with mom and dad in a particular situation. All of us have abundant creativity as children. We all can create and live our fantasies as if they were real—in fact, this is what makes them become real.

As we grow older, we become more and more serious about life's responsibilities and exchange our creativity for realistic things. All the fun of creativity goes out the window.

We must get our early-age creativity back in order to have fun creating joy in our lives. If we create situations that we like, we are going to be able to enjoy those situations just as we did when we were kids.

Part of our tension is the seriousness of adulthood that we impose on ourselves. This attitude brings us boring and pressuring conditions in life. Because of this mentality, we go looking for opportunities while full of fear and insecurity, instead of thinking of that particular situation as an opportunity for fun.

The "richest" people in the world were smart enough to look for some creative thing that they love to do. When I say, "rich," I mean emotionally, spiritually, physically and mentally. The combination of love for something + creativity = success. Of course, not 100% of us become successful with everything we create, but the fact that it's so much fun gives us a boost, and we keep working on it until we get it right, or if necessary, we can create something new that is also fun.

Taking risks is fun, and allows us to test our creative talents. It gives us a sense of freedom and helps us to give ourselves credit and support for our own efforts. To feel proud of our own doing is positive, and requires maturity on our part. To take risks for what we believe is adventurous and exciting for the creative mind.

The world was created because of a tremendous energetic force
We were created because the perfection of nature happened
Every material thing around us was created by humankind
Therefore we can also create our own visions and materialize them

To materialize our dreams we use our willpower
Mix it up with imagination and pleasure
Put water in to soften it up
Add some spice to excite
Keep on stirring until you feel it's right
Let it cook for time enough to solidify

After we mature, we finally get
All the rewards that time possesses
No doubt about it, it's compensating
To cook our visions with trust
and keeping on creating

For the awesome result of a positive factor
For choosing the best of our options
Believing in us against all matters
Trusting our instincts, intuitions and power
To bring results that matter and resolve

All those ingredients will bring flavor
To the outcome of a good creator
For the freedom of the warrior
For the beauty of it all

21

THE GAME

Concentration is a must for success in the game of life, as with any other game. There is no victory in a game if you are not focused. Learn the rules of life and play with intelligence and accuracy.

It helps also, to see this game as a learning process. If you don't win in the beginning, learn the lessons and avoid making the same mistakes next time. Keep on playing and become good at it, with confidence and knowledge. After awhile, we can reach the end of the line as champions, having learned clever strategies to help ourselves and others. Practice the game. Get your mind in shape for the exercises you engage in, day in and day out. Produce yourself as a great example for others, proving to you and to them, how important and how smart it is not to live in denial.

Confronting our demons is courageous and extremely clever at the same time. It aids in our evolution process. Credibility and points are added to our existential files for our efforts at improvement. In short, once we get the emotional health going, there will be enough motivation to get the other levels of healing (physical, mental and spiritual) going smoothly. Once we are emotionally fit, we can confront any kind of challenge with a reasonable attitude.

I compare my emotional awareness to the stubborn belly that I want to get rid of. The more exercise I push myself to do, the more positive results I get.

These lines are dedicated to those beginning these exercises:

I prefer to see life as a big game that we must know the rules to, in order to play.
I have to play many times, in order to know the tricks and nuances.
I must learn from my mistakes in order to get better at it.
I will be a really good player.
If I just don't give up and keep on playing,
I know one day I will win, because I insisted.
I am going to be a winner because I believe in me.
Because I will pay enough attention
Because I will practice a lot
Because even though I will lose many times
I will learn from my mistakes
Because I will want to win at
Life's tricky games

My reward will be
To regain the love of self
Someone made me lose
Back in time, in my childhood…

These lines are for those in the middle of their journey and exercises:

I see life as a big game that we must know the rules to, in order to play.
I played many times in order to know the tricks and nuances.
I learned from my mistakes in order to get better at it.
I became a real good player
Because I kept on playing it.

I knew one day if I played
I was going to win, because I insisted.
I was going to be a winner because I believed in me.

Because I paid enough attention
Because I practiced a lot
Because I lost many times
Because I learned from my mistakes
Because I wanted to win at
Life's tricky games

My reward was the love of self
Someone helped me to honor and learn
In the process of life since my childhood...

22

PROCRASTINATION

To Procrastinate—the dictionary defines this word as: "the act of keeping, delaying and putting things off." That means "not doing," which is to stagnate, no motion, no emotion—a clear example of not doing for yourself. Laziness? Perhaps. But definitely proof of lack of self-love, organization, emotional knowledge of self. No one I know who procrastinates is proud of doing so; they aren't proud of their lack of motivation, decision and determination. Discipline helps us humans to program and improve our conduct and expectations.

Decisions are not given to us; they are produced by us to improve our conditions in this lifetime. Therefore, we must face by all means, all the consequences of our actions. If we focus our attention on the end of the duty, we'll have the sense of pride only the winners get when they accomplish the end result. That action proves the determination and maturity of an individual.

These lines are dedicated to procrastinators:

I know I'm supposed to do what I promised.
I know I'm supposed to follow up.
No doubt I will do it eventually.
Eventually, casually and gradually.

But time is not on my side
It goes so fast and I didn't realize.

My intentions are good
I eventually will compromise.

Tomorrow I will do it
Because I said it so many times.
Of course, I know I can't prolong it.
It's so embarrassing sometimes.

Anyway, I couldn't do it
Because I had my reasons.
I had my troubles.
I couldn't function.
I couldn't finish.

Eventually, I will get there
And then I will stand proud
To finish my plans out
to complete my promises
and to allow solid words
to come about
combined with actions
for the sake of all.
Who knows?
Will I complete this project
In the fall?…

23

FREEDOM

Many people think that freedom is physical and/or financial, and, with that impression, they work, focusing on their goal. Many times we see propaganda using the following phrase: "Financial freedom for peace of mind."

There are also people who think that to be free is to have no money at all. Even though their statement is true, it is limited, because they are focusing only on the physical level.

The real deal is when we become aware of the four levels of healing, which will lead us to freedom. Believe it or not, the first road to genuine freedom is emotional freedom. Only when we reach this level will we be able to face, gain, or deal with the other levels in an intelligent and evolutionary manner.

If we manage to enter into a higher level of consciousness and self-awareness, where we know that we are unlimited in our ability to use the power of our minds to heal our bodies and our lives, we will understand that this healing power has never been outside of us, but has always been within.

We will move out of mass programming, mass thinking, and mass control, and move into individual self-awareness, individual power and individual freedom.

We are all of one mind and all healing is self-healing. Thoughts do heal. Everything that is physical around us was once a thought created in someone's mind. Therefore, everything that we can touch physically was created by another human mind with a purpose. There is no difference in us wanting to create healing for ourselves and for others. If our intent is projected with genuine belief, we can, and will, achieve what we set out to accomplish.

Freedom is something untouchable, but desired by most of us. Once we manage to get it, there's no going back to suffering or torment. The mind flies free as a bird in any direction we prefer, and it is always possible to realize our dreams on this level of awareness and higher Self-consciousness. This is what people from India call "Prana" and Catholics call "meeting with God."

24

EMOTIONAL SUCCESS STORIES

Dear Lygya:

Lygya, it is so important that you continue to offer this treatment to others. Everyone has dormant and unresolved issues that CAN be resolved without years of expensive therapy and finding other ways to medicate the pain—pain that we may not even know that we are carrying around and that affects the quality of our lives.

May you enjoy your continued success and receive blessings for your devotion and tireless effort in trying to help humanity find peace within ourselves and with the Creator. With all my love, dear friend…

Peace, L.B.

Hi Lygya,

And of course, I enjoyed your special gift again, which comes during the healings (smile).

Lygya, you are a remarkable person to get to know. It is always a pleasure to talk with you and to receive your guidance and insight. But most of all, it is beautiful how you care about all of us that you help and heal. Thank you so much!

Love,

Kelly Lucas

Lygya,

How are things? By the way, while I've had a bit of a relapse (following a one-month stay by my parents, who really affect the way I feel about myself), I still feel I benefited tremendously from your session. I left knowing a lot more about my emotional state than when I arrived.

Thanks very much

Chris

Hi Lygya,

It has been a week after the therapy and I really feel I need to give you a feedback—tremendously positive and a thankful feedback.

I feel free as ever in my life, I see life from a different perspective and I feel (sorry about so many "Feel" words) in a different dimension: THE PRESENT. Before I was living in an idealistic world, I was being a rebel with no cause. I am in a state of "before and after" at this moment of life. In the "before" phase my life was extremely overwhelmed with fear and that fear was in control of my life; now or in the "after" state my mind is so clear that I am completely able to decide who is going to be in control—not fear any more, but me.

Thank you for being part of my journey, for helping me to be reborn. I am very grateful to the universe for putting you on my way—finally you were the one who were able to put a stop to that blockage.

God bless you,

LUZ GALLEGO

D.E.A.R.

My experience with Lygya as a healer has been one of the most beneficial for me. My last session with her was extremely healing. I was having a fearful sensation in my solar plexus every morning when I got up and after our session, that feeling left my body. It's now 3 months, and I have not experienced that feeling anymore. It's just a wonderful experience to get up every morning and feel great! This is just one of the many benefits that I have experienced through Lygya's therapy. I highly recommend her to anyone that's looking to release emotional or mental blockages in their lives.

Have a great day!

Gianina

REIKI (one session)

Guess what..? I have two interviews on Monday...for work and since I have left you from having a little exchange of medicinal energy...the desperation and anger of money dissolved...and I realized that I never want to be depressed again...I was depressed for 15 years...NO MORE!! No, no honey...just thought you should know how I have transformed over night...

Juanita

DEAR (one session)

Hi there!

The depressive mode is much deeper than even I thought it was. However, I also think I have not slept enough in a long time. I'm going to sleep more (going = GONNA). I wish to go back to singing with others, and this is a way to start. Music is a key, so in that respect, I am going to bring music back to my life. It is a long road ahead. The treatment made me realize how much pain I am holding inside and how hard I continue to hold on to it. At least this is a step

Scot Sharr

HYPNOSIS

(Client with chronic physical pain. One session)

I don't remember when my knee started to hurt, it seems end-less...but I can remember after the one Hypnosis session I had with you, the chronic pain was actually gone girl!!!

Sandra Dudley

25

EMOTIONAL HEALING: HELPFUL MODALITIES

There are many different modalities of healing to help people with emotional blockages, such as, hypnosis, N.L.P., Rebirth, etc. It's up to us to research and find the modality and the healer that is the right one for us. There are cases in which people go through many modalities of healing before they can really tap into the deepest level of emotional healing.

The good news is, once we start to work on it, we are going to want more and more healing. We start to find points for improvement on many different levels, and start our life as a new process, with extreme new clarity. The feeling of victory each step of the way tells us that there is no going back. We will be sure, at last, that our personal power is going to take us wherever we want to go.

We must know our deep feelings and respect their causes, so we can treat and free them forever. We have feelings so that we may experience them—it's as simple as that.

I suggest that before beginning to use the various modalities, realize they will do nothing for us unless we believe we can, and will, improve our performance altogether. It's always up to US, not the healer. This is the responsibility of a lifetime—it's not to be taken for granted.

Only when we are willing to change for the better will the transformations begin to take place. It takes some time to get to the final results, but it's worth every single minute spent on healing the four bodies.

I suggest the modalities listed below to start the healing process. Don't hesitate to use any other modality you might find attractive. Do not get caught up in the money situation. Pay very deep attention to your instincts about charlatans in the business who just want to get by financially, as in any other profession. I am suggesting these techniques simply because I experienced them myself. If you feel attracted to other kinds of modalities, please go for it.

VITAL ENERGY (KI) treatment brings a 6,000 year-old ancient healing art to the west. It helps the flow of balanced energy in the body, releases pain and toxicity and restores natural health. It reconnects the individual with the cosmic life force energy. If you are interested in knowing more about the training process so that you can get more results from this incredible healing experience, don't hesitate to ask about the International Chun Do Sun Bup Training Center. The healer will touch your meridians (back and front), pressing them with the hands, in order to process a recycling of your energy.

REIKI is a laying-on of hands touch-healing system of incomparable ease and power. It is an energy attunement or initiation, which sets Reiki apart from every other form of laying-on of hands or touch healing. It opens and aligns our energy on the physical, emotional, mental and spiritual levels. The healer will hold her hands over different parts of the physical body, in order to apply the energy through the ancient symbols, as well as through psychic power, to begin the attunement process.

HYPNOTHERAPY uses hypnosis as a psychotherapeutic tool. The altered state that occurs under hypnosis has been compared to a state of deep meditation or transcendence, in which the innate recuperative abilities of the psyche are allowed to flow more freely. It can also be explained as a relaxed state of focused attention. It is a state during which the subconscious mind is open to suggestion to create positive change. Regression will take place, as well as progression, during a therapy session.

NLP (Neuro Linguistic Psychology) is an integration of neurology, psychology, linguistics, cybernetics, and systems theory. It is a technique to determine (neuro) thinking patterns (programming) by analyzing the (linguistic) actions of eye movement, breathing, and other body language. "Programming" refers to altering unconscious and harmful negative beliefs. Primarily using visualization techniques, the client will change the old mental code for a new one, developing more desirable, constructive behavioral patterns.

D. E. A. R. (Deep Emotional Alternative Release) is a shamanic healing process. It is Release and Transformational work. This technique releases emotional blockages through the energy centers (chakras). The goal is to guide the client through the subconscious mind to release blocked Emotions, such as traumas, anger, depression, and feelings of rejection, guilt, fears and insecurities and to lead them out of the physical body forever. This takes place in one session (in most cases). This technique also releases blockages through the energy centers (chakras). Everyone's path to emotional release is different. Dr. Lygya treats each person based on his or her individual needs.

The treatment length depends on each client, and usually takes three to four hours. This treatment is a combination of various modalities of alternative healing, such as Shamanism, (aromatherapy and chromotherapy), Reiki, Karuna Ki, Vital Energy, Deep Emotional Release BodyWork, Hypnosis and N.L.P.

For other modalities:

—visit your local health food store for free holistic magazines. See display ads

—search web sites for holistic health, emotional healing, therapy
—ask around

26

MY EMOTIONAL DISCOVERIES

When I first decided to be truthful with myself and deal with my demons and frustrations, I had no choice but to look within myself for the roots of my problems. I had a very poor childhood in Brazil. I was rejected by my father even before I was born, and then later on, when I was 9 years old, my mother and I became homeless in consequence of my father's disappearance. I grew up extremely insecure and thinking of myself as ugly physically and not so bright.

As a result of my childhood experiences, I grew up with insecurities about money and romance, as well as friendship; it always ended in disillusionment. I was always angry, my moods were always changing, I never trusted my partners and always felt the fear of losing them to other women. It was ironic that I got attracted to a lady's man, a selfish guy, an alcoholic, a cocaine addict, a pathological liar, and my last catch before my healing—a depressed and emotionally blocked sweetheart.

Throughout this wonderful, exciting life of a starving artist traveling around the world, I finally stopped in New York. After my divorce from the selfish man, I became so insecure about the financial aspect of my life that I suffered seven years of back injury. I had been a dance instructor and performing artist, and that physical condition was not helping at all. I started to think there was something wrong with me; my self-esteem was hitting the bottom.

The last straw was the rejection I was getting from my sweetheart and his Chinese family. His mother and father would not make a secret of the fact that I was not welcome into the family, because I was not Chinese. My psychological and physical pain was so excruciating, I could no longer take it, and I said to myself, 'Enough is enough! I got the first holistic magazine I could put my hands on, and called for help.

I was searching for outside help because my intellect knew I couldn't bear to deal with the heavy weight of the traumas I had alone. Going through the variety of healers' display ads, I selected three modalities that caught my attention and interest. One was the Deep Emotional Release BodyWork and the others were Past Life Regression with Hypnosis and spiritual channeling.

My experience with Past Life:
During the session I heard very clearly the name ALPHA OMEGA being said in a distant voice and I saw myself as a ball of light coming to Earth for the first time and arriving in the desert. (Now I know it was in Egypt). In the channeling session, I learned that my first experience as a human on earth was as a healer. I died then, due to the tremendous amount of treatment I was doing; healing and benefiting others without learning how to recycle my energy in order remain strong. That was my lesson to be learned in this lifetime. For this purpose, I met the Chundo Sunbup people from Korea, during a New Life Expo. I was attracted to them when I heard the heavy breathing and saw Master Ho and Master Kim together treating someone on the table. The light of these two wonderful beings was so bright and beautiful that I just could not avoid joining their temple, located in Manhattan.

This treatment helps the flow of balanced energy in the body, releases toxicity and restores natural health. At the same time, it reconnects the individual with the cosmic life force energy, as well as helping us to deal with our ancestors. After that learning experience, it took me a full year to feel ready to go out of the temple and practice on my own. My body ended up automatically doing the recycling method I had learned at any moment or in any situation. In that same year I went to Korea to visit the Temple and see the Grand Masters and their annual celebration of birth. The experience I had with the masters of the vital energy work is still vivid in my mind and heart. I have great admiration for them and truly love them unconditionally, for the rest of my life.

The Deep Emotional Release Bodywork, on the other hand, dealt with my deepest pain and traumas, taking me to a completely new dimensional level, about which I am writing now. The healer did a wonderful job in an hour, and I was so ready to free my pain, I surrendered and gave myself to the treatment as no one else would in such a short amount of time. I discovered later that one must be "ready" to go through this profound work.

As I evolved, I wanted to know more about everything in sight, related to healing. My curiosity intensified as I learned more and more about it. The more I experienced varied modalities of healing, the more I wanted to learn about them, and eventually, I became a walking book on the subject of healing.

LEARNING TO STOP MY CONTROLLING BEHAVIORS—

I got so excited about what I was learning that I got in trouble with some people for pressuring them with my healing beliefs. I thought that if I was a true healer, I was supposed to help every human being walking in my path. But I learned the hard way that I was also supposed to respect their freedom to choose if they are ready or not to be healed. That was one of my most difficult lessons to learn.

I used to try to change all my boyfriends' choices in life in terms of drugs, alcohol, depression etc. There are so many couples who argue with the same intention, without any results. I am mentioning this as an example, because a lot of couples work really hard on changing their mates without success. In the process, they get their feelings all fired up, ending up mad at one another, and eventually they separate.

I realized we are very eager to help to "change" that someone for positive purposes. My exercise is now the following: If that person doesn't show any interest in positive change in their life, I just have to let it go and change myself instead. If I don't, it proves to me that I am being a control freak.

I learned that we give help when someone is open to receive it—otherwise, it's our duty to learn how to let it go. Of course, if a situation calls for a discussion on the subject, I will mention different options for the seeker to choose. I still believe that for every person we meet there's a reason, and one never knows why that person is crossing our path. Our actions are lessons for us as well as for others—period!

As a result of my willpower efforts, today I am a Reiki &, Karuna KI Master, a Certified Hypnotherapist, and a Certified Master NLP Practitioner. I have a Doctoral degree in Alternative Healing and I am a member of the International Institute of Projectiology and Conscienciology, with the Science of Conscious Projection of our Astral Body. I also studied various meditation and Shamanic methods of healing, and I am about to invest in knowledge about Past Life Regression and get my Ph.D.

I also discovered in a Priestess Goddess workshop, that I have ISIS and BAST (ISIS, is the goddess of Civilization, Agriculture and Love, and BAST is the goddess of all arts, Music, Beauty and Joy), as my aliases in this third dimension. Therefore, in this lifetime, I represent Unconditional Love, Creation, Beauty and Joy. My Archangel name is Shinanim and my guard angel is Aralim.

I meditate and write (poems) every night and every time that I want to write a message of beauty and hope to someone. When I wake up in the morning, my first thought is that life is my friend, in all dimensions. My phone rings often with someone seeking help. They read my display ad in the local holistic magazines and call me for the same reason I called the two healers I chose in the past.

One of the best results of this incredible healing phenomenon is that even though I am a "foreigner," I feel confident enough to write these lines. Before my healing results, this idea was totally out of my reach. In fact, I used to beg friends to write things for me. Now I feel I must write and teach as a conduit for the regaining of power and the reconnection of the DNA force. Nothing will stop my power to touch millions of people, to help them to regain their power as I had the chance to do. My mission is to enjoy and share light, knowledge, beauty and love, indeed. All of us have the right to be happy eventually, without exception.

I might sound like a commercial, but I must say, so others have the chance to know, that I give my clients the time that was not given to me. I do not charge for my treatments by the hour; I believe each client has their own time clock, therefore they will have no pressure about time from me. The session takes as long as it's necessary to take. My satisfaction in helping people to regain their power is beyond words.

I am slowly working on my relationship with my mother, going through my childhood since the time I was conceived. Our relationship was always good for many reasons, but what is important is that we are going through the process of releasing old wounds.

Our lives were very difficult after my father deserted us, as my mother had only a high school education and she couldn't find a job that would give her a salary with which she could afford to raise me. Being homeless for a few years made us bond as friends and be supportive of one another.

Our incredible journey is a wonderful example of willpower, trust and honor between mother and daughter. Today I understand her fears and insecurities. I keep working on our relationship to help it to heal more and more, every time we have a phone conversation or whenever I go to Brazil to visit. We know we are meant to finish old business from past lives. We talk about it a lot.

The more I talk to my mother, the lighter and happier we feel about knowing each other on all levels. She no longer gets mad when I speak about things that I wouldn't dare to in the past. Now she listens and respects me as a human being, seeing beyond the child that did not know what to say or do. (That is what she used to say to me all the time: "What do you think you are? You don't know everything.")

I am mature enough to point out personal things to my mother in a respectful, and even humorous, manner. So, we both delight ourselves in endless memories for the joint experience of living and expressing our deep feelings on a higher level. If I could help all my clients to go through what I am going through with my mom, I would.

Many people go on with their lives, taking their parents' lives for granted. It is worth a shot…Humor is a good way to start a deep conversation without putting the other person on the defensive. I say, 'After the smile, go for the blow,' with positivity and diplomacy, of course.

Our parents are the first immediate life challenge we face in order to evolve. It is wise to understand the way they act, because they also had a hard time with their own parents and with society. This experience is good for us, in order to help us to mature and see beyond our limitations.

My real father is apparently deceased. I searched around after 25 years, in order to contact him again, but with no luck. I was working on my relationship with him for the longest, meditating and visualizing him, until one day I saw a TV movie that touched me deeply. (There was a scene where the father was dancing with the daughter.) A tremendous amount of sadness come over me at that moment, and because of my emotional knowledge, I let it go. As a result, I had an incredible amount of release from past frustration and from longing feelings that evening.

The compulsive cry came from the fact that I allow myself to surrender to my emotions about not having my beloved father dancing with me, or seeing me dancing and singing—ever. As a result, I had the most wonderful dream I ever had about my dad—dancing and laughing at an event where I later sang for him. I believe my dream was a sign that he sent me to let me know he also loves me and cares.

The feeling of emptiness that my father left in my heart was, in the past, overwhelming. I mixed my sadness with anger, and later on became very depressed, addicted to sugar, sick with various allergies, and totally careless about money. Every time I would make money, I would spend it on clothes, food, dining out, jewelry, and whatever else I would feel attracted to, as if I was making up for my poor childhood, or for my lack of love.

A few years after my emotional healing, I decided to respect what money symbolizes and brings to our material life and comfort. Now I am also working on my financial knowledge and glad there are smart options for investing. For an immigrant, artist, Latin, Black, Third World native, with a little English grammar, I managed to write well enough to get a Doctoral degree and earned my Ph.D.

As an alternative doctor, I want to make sure the client will feel at ease on this journey. I open and align the client's energy with a Reiki & Karuna KI treatment, in order to deeply relax the client on the physical, mental, spiritual and emotional levels. The vital energy work of Korea helps to cleanse the physical body of "intruders" (entities from the second and first dimensions) and meridians blockages. Then the

Deep Emotional Alternative Release will target the subconscious mind and chakras to release old traumas. This is followed by Hypnotherapy and NLP.

My intention is to free my clients from unwanted patterns at once, in one single session. A few clients decide to come back for a second treatment on their own. I don't like to influence them to arrange for a second session, simply because I believe in my clients' decisions. One of my goals is to have my clients believing in themselves and taking charge of their lives. They have to know or not, whether they need another session. Some of us just can't surrender deeply enough in order to allow the pain to come to the surface in the first session. That is why, a few weeks later, a few of them realize they have another layer that needs to be taken care of, and they will call me. This treatment is that powerful.

Our consciousness is becoming reconnected to our DNA. We are realizing that in addition to physical, mental and spiritual healing, the emotional level needs to be healed as well, in order to complete the circle of life free of blockages.

Healing is my mission on earth. I am honored and grateful to the forces of the universe for their guidance in my learning experiences.

I also learned that there is no warrior without a war. There are solutions in every problem. There are always two sides of the coin for every challenge. There is always a choice of using optimism instead of pessimism in life situations. In short, it's up to us to take responsibility for our decision to be alive.

27

EMOTIONAL EXERCISES

Because our physical body is made of dense energy and our other bodies of lighter and different kinds of energies, we can explore many different exercises and pleasurable things to do to play with our minds, power, emotions and much more. The only thing that limits us is our lack of knowledge about exploring other worlds, dimensions and feelings.

On the physical level, we can explore several ways to release energy and gain pleasure. We can do things such as dance, play a musical instrument, write, sing, speak, joke, play a sport, etc...All these can help us to cope with pressure and physical tension. On the other hand, we can navigate other dimensions with meditation and conscious out-of-body experiences, visualization, self-hypnosis, and more.

Those types of exercises are important because they deal with our inner self. In other words, our physical bodies, as well as our minds, are actively involved in the process, rather than what happens when we watch TV or movies and our physical body stagnates for hours. These distracting actions limit us to exercising only one part of us—our minds. It's okay to do that, but not only that. We've got to find emotional balance in our exercises, in order to evolve on many different levels. Many of us do this naturally, but some of us don't feel as inspired or motivated, for whatever reason. It may be due to lack of self-esteem, or insecurity of some sort.

It is a must to look for the right teacher, guide or sign that will take us on the road to achievement, pride, discipline, well-being and happiness. Eventually, our search for power will be rewarded, and we can regain our power at last.

Conscious emotional exercise is a discipline that I have been practicing for awhile with lots of success. Practice as much as possible, every day, every time, every minute, every second. Be aware of what you are doing and why, observe how the actions you take influence you to attract light or darkness. That way, we learn how to learn the lessons. If it's not a good, pleasurable outcome or experience, we don't repeat ourselves. This process will help us to create a friendly environment around ourselves. Once that is done, we start to see the changes made around us and the way people begin to treat us. We will be happily surprised at how much we have changed for the better and how worthy our efforts were.

Understanding ourselves and others, and consequently, forgiving ourselves and others, can be a tough task to accomplish; particularly if our actions involved rudeness, bad intentions or misbehavior we know was harmful to others. It's important to mention here that none of us should be too quick to judge actions, because we all have reasons for doing what we do. One may never know what happened to that offender in his or her childhood; why they are the way they are; if they were abused by society or rejected by a parent, and find the anger/pain is too overwhelming to bear. There is a reason for everything, even if we don't agree with it. This applies also to judging ourselves. Being patient with ourselves helps the process of understanding and keeps the power of the situation in check. It's a good exercise for understanding others' actions, as well.

If we get used to the idea of improving each day, every chance we can, we will get what we want eventually, guaranteed. Sometimes it takes a while for us to get there, just as some babies take longer to walk or talk;

we also have different time frames for accomplishing our tasks. The most important thing is that we keep on doing it, and don't give up on ourselves. I am living proof of what I preach. Every day, in every moment, my internal dialogue is about positive things and changes that have to be made for the better. It became fun and exciting to me to be able to gain power over my old bad habits of sugar craving, overeating, excessive shopping, incessant talking, seeking the acceptance and affections of boyfriends and friends, obsessive concern about money to survive, overdependence on respect and consideration from others, along with depression and loneliness.

Because I am very stubborn, it took a while for me to digest and feel at ease with my bad habits and lack of self-esteem. Every day before I go to bed, I write about my day with a positive message of learning in mind. The messages come in poetry form, so I know eventually I will organize and publish them as an example of how we can use stubbornness to our advantage, as well as anger, anguish and desperation. Every morning I motivate myself to be productive in many ways. It's fun to wake up with creative ideas and to work on them. I realized that it was fun to be alone to experience my own limitations and to take responsibility for my life into my own hands. I created a constant curiosity about the human mind, emotion, and spiritual levels, as I already knew about the physical so well.

The challenge of winning at physical competition is a thrill that makes most people excited and eager to accomplish. We are competitive by nature, and that takes some of us to incredible achievements, sometimes even hard to believe. In some instances, we know what was possible because we saw it with our own eyes on TV, or personally. There is no difference in their physical bodies. (They have one head, neck, chest, two arms, two legs, etc.) The willpower of those competitors is the point; they are so focused and so motivated to win at all costs, that eventually they will. They simply don't give up on their dreams or themselves. That's the true winner at all levels. The power of their minds provides the drive. We all can do that if we trust ourselves enough.

So, from this minute on, exercise your mind to WIN. In every minute, you can remember that you are winning. And if you can visualize that scene in your mind every day and every minute, eventually you will win. Write about it, talk about it, act on it—that's the goal. If you feel all alone sometimes, take a walk to a health food store. Pick up a holistic magazine for free, and search for free or paid seminars or workshops offering what attracts you the most. Meet new people—those who, like you, are searching for their accomplishments. Of course they will relate to you! Make new and positive friends; reprogram your mind with only positive stuff. Get rid of the negative old thoughts as they come. Be a winning warrior of your own personal war!

These exercises will help you to access the deeper knowledge of your soul. They address many of the following…

EMOTIONS, EXPERIENCES AND STATES OF BEING:

FRUSTRATION	JOY
INSECURITY	LOVE
LONELINESS	SUCCESS
BOREDOM	ABUNDANCE
SADNESS	CONTRIBUTION
ANGER	FLEXIBILITY
IMPATIENCE	CREATIVITY
ANNOYANCE	POWER
ANXIETY	
ASSURANCE	CURIOSITY
	UNDERSTANDING

GUILT	BEAUTY
UNWORTHINESS	SPIRITUALITY
DEPRESSED	SINCERITY
DISRESPECT	INTEGRITY
HUMILIATION	KINDNESS
CONFIDENCE	
ECSTASY	

EXERCISES

Exercise #1: THE CAUSE (CHECKING THE CAUSE OF BEHAVIOR)

WRITE DOWN ON A PIECE OF PAPER THE FOLLOWING:

a) HOW YOU FEEL (HONESTLY) ABOUT CERTAIN THINGS THAT ARE MAKING YOU UNHAPPY. TAKE A LOOK AT YOUR PATTERNS, THINGS THAT YOU SEE HAPPENING IN YOUR LIFE OVER AND OVER AGAIN. EXAMPLE: RELATION-SHIPS, EATING DESORDERS, COMPULSIVE SHOPPING, SMOKING, ETC.

b) GO BACK TO THE FIRST DAY YOU REALIZED YOU STARTED TO DO EACH ONE. WRITE IT DOWN. (THEN DEAL WITH THAT THE BEST WAY YOU CAN, ENERGETI-CALLY. IF YOU FEEL IT'S TOO MUCH TO BEAR BY YOUR-SELF, SEEK HELP FROM HEALER IN THE FIELD; THERE ARE GOOD ONES AND BAD ONE. SEARCH AND PAY ATTEN-TION TO YOUR INTUITION, RESPECT YOUR RED FLAGS (LIKE A BAD FEELING). IF YOU HAVE DOUBTS, DON'T DO IT. GO ELSEWHERE, BUT GET HELP. SOMETIMES SURREN-DERING AND GETTING THE NECESSARY HELP IS ALL THAT WE NEED TO BEGIN A COMPLETELY FULFILLING AND WONDERFUL LIFE.)

c) CHECK AND SEE THE RELATION BETWEEN THE HABIT AND THE CAUSE

Exercise #2: TRANSFORM (LEARN & ATTRACT POSITIVE BEHAVIOR)

1st round:
a) WRITE DOWN A LIST OF THINGS THAT YOU DO BUT YOU DON'T LIKE
b) WRITE DOWN A LIST OF THINGS (ON A SEPARATE PIECE OF PAPER) THAT OTHERS DO IN RELATION TO YOU THAT YOU DON'T LIKE
c) COMPARE THE LISTS

2nd round:
a) WRITE DOWN A LIST OF THINGS THAT YOU NEED TO DO IN ORDER TO CHANGE THE THINGS YOU DON'T LIKE TO DO (ON A SEPARATE PIECE OF PAPER)
b) WRITE DOWN A LIST OF THINGS THAT YOU NEED TO DO IN ORDER TO CHANGE PEOPLE'S ATTITUDES TOWARDS YOU FOR THE POSITIVE

Exercise #3: MAKING PLANS (SUCH AS A PLAN TO MAKE MONEY OR A PLAN TO BECOME A "LOVENNAIRE"!!!)

PLAN #1: MAKE A PLAN TO ACHIEVE A BETTER RELATION-SHIP WITH THE SELF? TAKE IT SERIOUSLY. USE THE INFORMATION ABOVE TO CREATE NEW GOALS FOR TRANSFORMATION.

PLAN #2: MAKE A PLAN TO ACHIEVE HAPPINESS (EMO-TIONAL HEALTH)

PLAN #3: MAKE A PLAN TO ACHIEVE SPIRITUAL HEALTH

PLAN #4: MAKE A PLAN TO ACHIEVE PHYSICAL HEALTH

PLAN #5: MAKE A PLAN TO ACHIEVE MENTAL HEALTH

PLAN #6: MAKE A FRESH MAP EACH DAY WITH ONE ITEM OF EACH PLAN MENTIONED ABOVE. WRITE DOWN THE WAYS TO GET WHERE YOU WANT TO GO, STEP BY STEP. BE FOCUSED AND MOTIVATED. MAKE THIS PROCESS PLAYFUL FUN. YOU CAN BE CREATIVE AND USE YOUR INTELLIGENCE TO GET WHAT YOU WANT AND THEN FEEL PROUD.

MAKE THE PLANS AND THE MAP THE MOST READBLE MATERIAL YOU FOCUS YOUR ATTENTION ON. READ THEM AS MUCH AS POSSIBLE. FOLLOW UP.

TAKE YOUR LIFE SERIOUSLY. IT IS A MATTER OF LIFE AND DEATH, REALLY!

EVERY EMOTION HAS A MESSAGE.

SEVEN WAYS YOU COULD APPROACH AN EMOTIONAL SITUATION

1. IDENTIFY WHAT THE EMOTION IS

2. AKNOWLEDGE AND APPRECIATE THE MESSAGE THE EMOTION IS SENDING TO YOU. LEARN FROM IT. ASK YOURSELF WHY YOU ARE FEELING THAT WAY.

3. GET CURIOUS ABOUT WHAT IT IS OFFERING YOU. HOW COULD YOU USE IT TO MAKE YOU, OR IT, BETTER? DO YOU NEED TO CHANGE THE WAY YOU'RE ACTING? CLARIFY WHAT YOU WANT. MAYBE YOU ARE HOLDING ON TO THE SAME OLD PATTERNS, MAYBE IT'S A GOOD OPPORTUNITY TO CHANGE FOR THE BETTER. MAYBE IT

WOULD BE GOOD TO CHALLENGE YOURSELF A BIT. PLAY THE GAME.

4. REASSURE YOURSELF. HAVE YOU FELT THIS EMOTION BEFORE? IF SO, HOW DID YOU GET THROUGH IT? WAS IT A GOOD OR BAD DECISION? COULD IT HAVE BEEN IMPROVED? FIND OUT WHEN YOU FELT THE SAME IN THE PAST, AS FAR BACK AS YOU CAN REMEMBER. WHAT DOES THAT ACTION OR NON-ACTION REMIND YOU OF?

5. USE YOUR EMOTIONS AS A WAY TO EMPOWERMENT. TEACH YOURSELF HOW TO BE IMPECCABLE INSIDE, RESPECT THE PERSON YOU ARE, DELIVER YOUR BEST PERFORMANCE FOR THE BEST PERSON IN THIS EXIST-ENCE—YOU!

6. PUT YOURSELF IN THE OTHER PERSON'S SHOES FOR A MOMENT. LITERALLY SEE YOURSELF GOING THROUGH LIFE AS THAT PERSON. WOULD YOU FEEL THE SAME AS THAT PERSON DOES? BE HONEST, FOR ONLY THEN WILL YOU BE ABLE TO UNDERSTAND THAT PERSON'S ACTIONS. THE FACT THAT YOU UNDERSTAND DOESN'T MEAN YOU HAVE TO AGREE WITH THEIR ACTIONS. BUT DO MAKE AN EFFORT TO SEE THEIR SIDE OF THE COIN.

7. TAKE ACTION, BE COURAGEOUS; TALK TO THE OTHER PERSON FROM YOUR HEART, WITH UNDERSTANDING, NOT WITH JUDGEMENT. IF YOU PROCEED IN THIS WAY, YOU'VE GOT THE FORMULA TO CHANGE YOUR WHOLE LIFE.

CHANGE YOUR PERSPECTIVE!

Unhealthy emotional states—we may experience:

AFRAID	HURT	POWERLESS	ANGRY
Appalled	Afflicted	Disbelieving	Annoyed
Awkward	Agonized	Depressed	Bitter
Cowardly	Crushed	Exhausted	Enraged
Dismayed	Distressed	Frustrated	Indignant
Doubtful	Despairing	Guilty	Infuriated
Lonely	Injured	Isolated	Irritated
Panicked	Sad	Numb	Offended
Restless	Suffering	Regretful	Resentful
Shaky	Tortured	Shamed	

EMOTIONS CAN BE USED AS SIGNALS FOR ACTION.

WE CAN CHOOSE TO USE THESE SIGNALS AS MESSAGES TO HELP IN CHANGING OUR UNHEALTHY FEELINGS.

1ST EXERCISE:

A good exercise for an unhealthy feeling is:

0. TAKE A DEEEEP BREATH

1. SURRENDER (ALLOW THE FEELING TO PROCESS. DON'T TRY TO CONTROL IT. LEARN FROM IT.

2. REMEMBER (WHAT IS IN THAT ACTION THAT REMINDS YOU OF OLD PAIN?)

3. ORGANIZE (BECAUSE OF THE WAY THE EMOTION IS PROCESSING. DETERMINE WHAT WOULD BE BETTER

FOR THE SITUATION; WHAT WOULD BE A SATISFACTORY RESULT FOR BOTH PARTIES?)

4. REACT POSITIVELY (RESPOND TO THE ACTION WITH A POSITIVE DIRECTION YOU DECIDE TO TAKE. MAKE SURE THAT THIS DECISION WILL BE GOOD FOR BOTH PARTIES. SO YOU CAN BE PROUD AND MATURE)

EXAMPLES:

FEEL REJECTED?

YOU CAN FEEL A LOT OF THINGS ALONG WITH THAT REJECTION. YOU MIGHT FEEL UNCOMFORTABLE, HURT, ANGRY OR LONELY. GO THROUGH THE LIST ABOVE AND SEE WHICH EMOTION IS PRIMARILY IN CONTROL. EXAMPLE: LET'S SAY YOUR PARTNER IS NOT GIVING YOU ENOUGH AFFECTION. YOU MIGHT FEEL...

UNCOMFORTABLE—FEELING SORRY FOR YOURSELF

1. SURRENDER (Feel deeply, check on the feeling that most contributed to your being in that situation.)

2. REMEMBER (Why is this sensation uncomfortable? Is that action or non action reminding you of an old situation?)

3. ORGANIZE (How could you get what you want as well as the other party? What could be a winner/winner situation?)

4. REACT (Express your solution, showing regard for the other party.) The same process applies to the following feelings:

FEAR—BEING ON ALERT

'GET READY SO WE CAN DEAL WITH SOMETHING THAT IS COMING UP!' IT IS THE MESSAGE OF WARNING. MOST

OF US BECOME FEARFUL AND TRY TO DENY IT OR WE SURRENDER TO THE FEAR AND INTENSIFY IT, INSTEAD OF GETTING PREPARED TO DEAL WITH THE APPROACHING PROBLEM.

HURT—CAN BE EXPECTATION OF LOSS ("THEY DON'T LOVE ME ANYMORE.") SEE WHAT HAS TO BE CHANGED. IS THIS AN APROPRIATE EMOTION TO FEEL AT THIS TIME, IN THIS SITUATION? MAYBE THE OTHER PERSON IS SIMPLY DISTRACTED AND YOUR PERCEPTION NEEDS TO BE CHANGED. YOU CAN ALSO CHANGE YOUR PRECEDURE.

ANGER—YOU HAVE A STANDARD FOR YOUR LIFE; SOME NEED THAT IS IMPORTANT TO YOU THAT IS NOT BEING MET BY ANOTHER PERSON, OR MAYBE IT'S NOT BEING MET BY YOU.

EXAMPLE: "PEOPLE DON'T RESPOND TO MY STANDARDS. MAYBE I NEED TO CHANGE MY PERCEPTION, BECAUSE NOT EVERYONE HAS TO ACT ACCORDING TO MY STANDARDS

PAIN—YOU NEED TO CHANGE THE WAY YOU LOOK AT THINGS. COMMUNICATE YOUR DESIRE TO SOMEONE OR BEHAVE IN A NEW WAY, ESPECIALLY IF THE PAIN INVOLVES SOMEBODY ELSE, OR CHANGES THE WAY YOU'RE TREATING OTHERS.

IF YOU IGNORE THE SIGNALS, THESE FEELINGS WILL ACCUMULATE, THE SIGNAL WILL INTENSIFY AND YOU'LL BECOME EVEN MORE ANGRY.

I MUST CHANGE MY EXPECTATIONS; THE WAY I AM EVALUATING LIFE; THE WAY I AM COMMUNICATING WHAT I NEED.

FRUSTRATION—YOU NEED TO CHANGE YOUR APPROACH TO ACHIEVE YOUR GOAL. WHATEVER YOU ARE GOING AFTER YOU'RE NOT GOING TO GET IT BASED ON THE WAY YOU ARE GOING ABOUT IT. YOU'RE TRYING TO GET THE A NEW RESULT BY DOING THE SAME THING OVER AND OVER AGAIN. YOUVE GOT TO CHANGE YOUR APPROACH. YOUR PERCEPTION AND PROCEDURE.

DISAPPOINTMENT—MAYBE YOU HAVE TOO HIGH AN EXPECTATION. YOU'VE SET STRONG GOALS WITHIN A CERTAIN TIME FRAME. MAYBE YOU WANT TO CHANGE YOUR GOALS

OR BE CREATIVE WITH TIME AND REALITY. COME UP WITH A NEW OUTCOME

GUILT—YOU VIOLATED ONE OF YOUR OWN STANDARDS. DON'T DENY IT! NEITHER EMBRACE IT AS IF THIS IS THE ONLY THING THAT MATTERS. WHATEVER YOU DID, YOU DID IT FOR A REASON. DEAL WITH IT MATURELY AND GET THE MESSAGE THAT YOU NEED TO CHANGE SOMETHING. GO BACK, CLEAR IT UP, CHANGE THE WAY YOU SPOKE TO SOMEONE, APOLOGIZE, ETC. ANY OF THESE ACTIONS WILL CLEAR UP THE GUILT.

IN THIS WAY GUILT SERVES A GOOD PURPOSE: IT HELPS TO MAKE US A BETTER PERSON, A MORE MATURE PERSON. IT KEEPS US ON TRACK.

INADEQUACY—A NEED TO GET BETTER AT SOMETHING. GO OUT AND PRACTICE GETTING BETTER.

OVERLOADED—A SIGNAL TO REEVALUATE WHAT IS MORE IMPORTANT.

A) WRITE DOWN IN THE ORDER OF PRIORITY WHAT IS ABSOLUTELY IMPORTANT. WHAT IS A NECESSITY TO YOU, AS OPPOSED TO A DESIRE.

B) PUT THEM IN ORDER OF PRIORITY.

C) TAKE THE FIRST THING ON THE LIST AND DO SOMETHING ABOUT IT. CHUNK DOWN.

LONELINESS—We NEED A CERTAIN CONNECTION WITH CERTAIN PEOPLE. WHAT KIND OF CONNECTION? IN WHICH WAY do I WANT TO BE WITH SOMEONE? IT CAN BE A SEXUAL CONNECTION OR JUST TALKING TO SOMEONE.

3RD EXERCISE

GET TO THE POINT WHERE YOU FEEL THE FOLLOWING AUTOMATICALLY:

1. BE IN A LOVING AND WARMING STATE

2. BE APPRECIATIVE AND GRATEFUL

3. GET CURIOUS. WONDER ABOUT LIFE AND OTHERS. STUDY MORE ABOUT YOURSELF.

4. GET EXCITED AND PASSIONATE EVERY DAY! YOU'RE ALIVE, ENJOY! DECIDE TO FEEL GOOD. IT'S YOUR CALL, YOU DECIDE TO BE THIS WAY OR NOT.

5. DETERMINATION. DISCIPLINE

6. BE MORE FLEXIBLE. DON'T BE JUDGMENTAL ABOUT OTHERS. PEOPLE ALWAYS DO THE BEST THEY CAN WITH THE RESOURCES THEY HAVE.

7. CONFIDENCE. FAITH. TRUST.

8. BE CHEERFUL. HAVE A SENSE OF HUMOUR. LAUGH. BE SILLY.

9. GET HEALTHY.

10. CONTRIBUTE TO SOCIETY.

4TH EXERCISE:

1. WRITE DOWN A LIST OF ANYTHING THAT MAKE YOU FEEL GOOD THAT HAS NO NEGATIVE EFFECT. EXPAND YOUR CHOICES AND PUT THEM IN ORDER OF PREFERENCE.

2. LISTEN TO MUSIC YOU LIKE, EAT DELICIOUS HEALTHY MEALS, EXERCISE, DANCE, SING, HAVE SEX, GO TO THE PARK.

3. NOTHING IN LIFE HAS ANY MEANING EXCEPT THE MEANING YOU GIVE IT.
IF YOU DON'T LIKE THE WAY YOU FEEL, CHOOSE TO CREATE A NEW MEANING.

4. HAVE FUN WITH YOUR EMOTIONS; LEARN FROM THE ONES THAT ARE PAINFUL. PLAY WITH THEM LIKE A CHILD WHO IS DISCOVERING THE FUN IN HAVING DREAMS AND WHO FINDS HAPPINESS IN THE SIMPLE THINGS IN LIFE.

28

DOCUMENTED HEALING SESSIONS

It is important to realize that the cases in this book hit only the highlights. I am skipping the intimate aspect to protect the privacy of others. I am also changing all names for the same reason. The case histories in this book represent a small percentage of people I've helped during the past six years. They represent what I remember, as I don't allow tapes recorders in the D.E.A.R sessions, because of the distraction this can create. What follows is a description of the facts with the results. My intention here is to educate the general public about these sessions and their positive results.

Case#1

Problem: Guilt

Marie came to me for healing because of problems with her professional and personal life. She felt guilty about having everything easy, while her friends, on the contrary, did not. To fill that gap of confidence she decided to sabotage her life, not allowing herself to succeed, so she would be like the friends around her.

Marie was my Emotional Release Body Work client in 1997. She was also a very close friend of mine.

Marie is very active socially, taking care of a society, being supportive of friends who always had parties at her place. She would not think twice to help a friend in any case in which she was required to do so. She used to live with the man of her dreams for a long time and he was also a very friendly and easy-going guy.

My approach was to go straight to her childhood, where she grew up apparently very happy, having everything she could possibly want. Going through the process of regression to childhood, I got Marie to tell me about a sexually abusive situation in her childhood. She had never told anyone about it for her own reasons, and until today, she has connection with the abusive person, without saying a word.

The healing process took about three hours. I used questions to target the subconscious mind in order to be able to find the cause of Marie's guilt about the good things she had in life.

By questioning her feelings at the time and now, her reactions and behavior, I went through the process of releasing Marie's guilt and feelings of complicity with her abusive family member.

Being very charming and sophisticated, Marie got a lot of attention from men and women in general. She was also a leader. After the treatment, Marie's behavior changed:

—She began to question her friends, friendships and devotion to the society of support they created.
—She felt like she was the only one really pulling it together.
—She began to tire of the situations in which she put herself.
—She discovered a new profession and began to study with passion
—She decided to get married months later
—She became more protective of her time and energy

Two years later she moved from her old apartment, got married, and received a brand new car as a gift from her husband and mom. She no longer contacted me as she used to.

Case#2

Problem > Chronic Fatigue Syndrome

At first I didn't think Larat was going to get to my place. The impression I had over the phone was that she was physically exhausted, but still fighting for positive transformation. That's what I look for in a client. If they believe that healing is important, they have my support.

I always tell my clients over the phone before sessions, that they are the leaders of the healing process. The combination of energy around us, (my 100% intent and the client's 100% intent, making 200%) will make the process successful.

At that time I used Shamanic and D.E.R.B. modalities to treat Larat, as it was all I knew.

Here it is her letter, written about one year after the treatment. (One session)

> Dear Lygya:
>
> We became connected a year ago when I responded to your advertisement for Emotional Release Body Work. (It was your eyes that caught my attention in your picture!) At that time, I was clinically diagnosed with depression, which affected every area of my life. I was hitting rock bottom. Symptoms of chronic fatigue, hopelessness, low self-esteem, and lack of energy affected my ability to function in daily activities. As a result, I almost lost my job due to chronic lateness and an inability to complete assignments on time, as I was always exhausted. I lost valuable friendships because I was unable to maintain consistent contact with my friends. I was so tired physically and emotionally that I ran home to sleep every chance that I could.

Ten years of my life had passed trying to fight the depression through therapy. The therapy addressed some surface issues, but I knew I needed a trusted spiritual approach to resolve this illness. Spirit led me to you during my search for alternatives.

A year later, my depression has been lifted after our one and only session. The bodywork treatment allowed me to address deep-rooted unresolved issues that I carried and was unaware of. Lygya, you helped me face my inner fears in such a professional, non-judgmental and supportive way. As you guided me thorough the treatment, I understood how my issues affect my life and interactions with others.

Moreover, you confirmed that my emotional cleansing would manifest through new changes in my life over the next year. I can't believe it! I have made so many accomplishments. I returned to school, improved significantly in punctuality at work, and have been able to keep all of my commitments. My interactions with others have also improved tremendously.

There's a new glow that radiates from me and an increased confidence to take on life's challenges, as I have so much more energy to do so. People are drawn to me and family and remaining friends comment on the drastic, positive change in my persona.

Lygya, it is so important that you continue to offer this treatment to others.

Everyone has dormant and unresolved issues that CAN be resolved without years of expensive therapy and finding other ways to medicate the pain. Pain that we may not even know that we carry and affect the quality of our lives. May you enjoy your continued success and receive blessing for your devotion and tireless effort in trying to help humanity find peace within ourselves and with the Creator. With all my love, dear friend...

Peace,
L.B.

Case #3

Problem > Afraid of success, nervous, shortness of breath.

Paul was a technician for many years. His primary fears were fear of success and public speaking. I began the session by asking him to fill out a questionnaire, and afterwards, I invited him to sit on my new wonderful deluxe massage chair. After 10 minutes of massage therapy, Paul was invited to begin a shamanic ritual for financial abundance. In the Shamanic ritual, I lit a candle, performed Reiki on a big crystal I keep on my altar for my Shamanic rituals, prepared the sage, sweet grass and an Egyptian powder incense for cleansing. I told Paul to hold his money and crystal together in his hands, for concentration and intent to attract money into his life. After Paul was guided to the massage table, I told him to breath in a certain manner until I finish cleansing myself and the environment.

After giving Reiki, Vital Energy and DERB treatments, I added Hypnosis, Regression and NLP techniques in order to enhance my client's abilities to heal his fear.

After asking verbal permission to touch his physical body, I used Reiki to deeply relax him (the client had a hard time relaxing) and Vital Energy to recycle the old energy for new. Only then did I begin the Deep Emotional Release, which was hard to work with in the beginning, as Paul had a hard time remembering the past, which is necessary in order to release the old feelings.

Paul was traumatized when he was about five or six years old, when a schoolteacher had him stand up and read for the class. He was very nervous and could not read the words clearly. He felt frustrated and embarrassed.

In order to help him remember what triggered his behavior, I hypnotized him. After inducing relaxation, I told him I was going to count from ten to one and that when I got to one, he would be five years old. He did follow my instructions and the treatments proceeded smoothly for the remaining time. I used NLP for the reprogramming of his mind, and I anchored him by having him visualize himself speaking to an audience. Under my command he also heard, saw and felt the audience's applause after a public speaking event and he heard people asking questions afterwards. I used audio because Paul was mainly an audio person.

The treatment took about four hours. I consider this treatment a successful one because of Paul's reaction after I finished. Not only had his breathing improved, he was very relaxed and his speech was extremely clear.

To finalize the session, I suggested he read two books, *Creative Visualization* and *Power Speech*.

Paul said good-bye, giving me a big hug with a wonderful smile.

Case #4

Problem > Lack of self-confidence, courage to speak out, to say no,

This client is one of the three clients who came back for a treatment. In her letter we can see the difference between the sessions and how she perceives her life now. When Kelly came to me, she was shy and insecure. The first treatment showed me the dominant mother and the struggle Kelly had to go through to survive and learn how to speak out on her own behalf.

> Hi Lygya,
>
> First off, I would like to thank you for being the loving, kind person that you are. The way God manifested you has made it possible for me to show you both my love and my pain without reservation or fear of judgment.

I came to you after two healings. Although there was a great deal of releasing that came from these sessions, they were primarily pulling away from me the events that were surrounding me at the time. These sessions with others brought me to a state where I was no longer confused about the events occurring in my life at the time.

But of course, my first session with you—deep emotional release—was just that. You and I went to the core of the pain I was feeling. I released and healed the events in my life that initiated the painful situations that came about later in my life. I was able to recognize my own energy and feelings vs. the feelings others had projected towards me. I was able to forgive and share moments where I could reconcile unfinished business with others. And when we where done with our first session, I went home feeling reborn.

This energy had left me bright, and giddy and childlike. I felt pure. This was so obvious that one of the conductors on Metro North noticed and asked me if I was born again. :) Of course the answer was yes! From that point, I was empowered and able to rationalize with my loved ones, without feeling drained by them. Especially when others used their emotions/energies to manipulate mine. I was able to free myself from that. I was able to lovingly maintain my own sensibilities throughout emotional negotiations with others. Finally, I was able to do this and still share with the people I love, the love that they needed.

My second request for a session came about because I am preparing for a new stage in my life. I am looking forward to having a family, and relocating. With this I wanted to bring my clearest consciousness to the children I'm looking forward to having, and to the husband I'm excited about sharing the rest of my life with. I wanted again to energize the purity I had felt through that first session.

I wanted to ensure that no/or at least minimal negativity would follow me into the next stage of my life. Our second session helped me to confirm my feelings about the next steps in my life. And interestingly enough, where my first session focused on the female influences on my behavior, this session focused on the male influences. This session was much more joyful. And, we also included a new addition to the healing—hypnosis. It showed me how much I had healed, and how far I had developed as a soul. And of course, I enjoyed your special gift again which comes during the healings (smile). Lygya you are a remarkable person to get to know. It is always a pleasure to talk with you and receive your guidance and insight. But most of all it is beautiful how you care about all of us that you help and heal. Thank you so much!

Love,
Kelly Lucas

Case#5

Problem > Insecurity, no romantic relationship

Kit is a personal friend, wonderful singer and person. She came to me because she was looking for a personal improvement, nothing specific. At that time she had Shamanic and DERB treatments only. During the treatment I discovered that Kat felt rejected by her mother all her life. I helped her to see, feel and hear that the feeling of being rejected by her mom guided her through life, causing her to feel less than she was, as well as causing lack of self love. Besides using chakra release as one of the processes, I also guided the client to visualize a favorite place where she would feel empowered and relaxed. There she should see, feel and talk to her mother and resolve old issues she never had the chance or courage to verbalize.

The session was very successful. At the end I asked what else she would like to work on that day to improve her life. She said that she would like to find her soul mate.

Last October Kat got married to a wonderful man (a musician and also a friend of mine), gave life to a health and beautiful baby boy and is happy at last.

It is very curious that I was divided between the two weddings of my most dear friends—*on the same day!* They don't know one another nor knew about one another's wedding dates.

I am also struck by the fact that they were treated at the same time of the year in 1998.

Kat married in the morning in Boston and Marie in upper Manhattan in the evening. They were both finally happy and so was I.

Case#6

Problem > lack of money, no romance

Moran is the only client that came four times for treatment. She is a real estate agent and tells me that she feels she has layers of issues to be healed.

She was rejected by both parents and was raised by her grandmother. Her father died away from her (she refused to go to see him) and her mother rarely told her she loved her. When she did say it, it sounded to her daughter as if were untrue.

She grew up having been taught that money was very difficult to get, as well as not having someone to share her life with.

For three sessions, I used Shamanic, Reiki, Vital Energy and DERB on the subject. During the fourth session I began using Hypnosis and NLP techniques, which helped her to focus on the two issues she most wanted to.

In the middle of the last session I used an induction for relaxation, with breathing techniques, after asking if romance or financial freedom was her primary goal. She chose financial freedom. Moran came to the conclusion that worrying about money would not help her in her relationship, therefore she preferred to work on the financial aspect. I asked her how much money she would like to make and deposit in her account. First she said $5,000 and I suggested she imagine money enough to by all things she would like to have. Moran then responded with "$100,000."

I used NLP techniques and asked her to see herself on a big movie screen with a $100,000 check in her hands walking towards the bank to deposit it. I guided her in every single detail until she could see the receipt in her hands.

As this is a very special case, I do not know yet if Moran met with success in her financial dreams or her dreams of romance, but I will know eventually. The important thing in this case is that Moran never came back for the same reason. She knows and is perfectly all right about the layers of healing she has to go through in order to accomplish her goals in this lifetime.

Case #7

Problem > Lack of professional confidence teaching and relationship with students

With tears in her eyes, Cynthia told me that she was thinking about giving up her career as a teacher. She was teaching teenagers at the time.

She was one of my old clients and Shamanic and DERB modalities were applied in her treatment. She felt rejected by her mother and didn't grow up with the father. Her mother was very competitive with her and she didn't feel strong enough or capable of professional success.

Because of her mother's comments and lack of support, the subject had a lack of self-confidence. After she released a great deal of anger and frustration, I guided the client through the love and forgiveness part of the treatment, visualizing her mother and communicating her frustrations and expectations. I programmed the subject for self-love, asking if she was willing from now on to do whatever was in her power to succeed in this life time.

Her answer was yes.

I remember seeing her about three or so months later. It seemed as if she had "happiness" written on her forehead. Her smile was so vivid, I became really curious. I casually asked how she was she doing with her students. Cynthia's answer was very casual as well, she smiled and said that everything was just terrific and her students were fine, she was having a lot of fun with them etc. I was very surprised, because she did not give me any sign that she remembered the treatment she had with me; it was as if her subconscious mind had completely erased the information from her consciousness.

Since all I cared about was the fact that she succeeded on her quest for recognition by her students as a teacher, I did not go into detail or ask any further questions. I just felt good about having the confirmation: one more person being helped by the treatment to accomplish their goals.

Case#8

Problem > Anger and lack of self-love

Seta approached me for treatment about a year ago. Her first issue was anger and she was one of the few clients that never cried during treatment. She resented her grandmother for her prejudice against her. Seta overheard her grandmother's racist comment about her one day. Also, she had always felt overprotected by her mother and grandmother; she felt that they didn't really respect her opinions or intelligence.

These experiences resulted in a very angry person, with a complete dislike of herself physically, to the point where she had never had a romance—ever!

This case is special in regards to my intense follow-up with her. She approached the subject several times afterwards and the more we talked about it, the more we saw improvement on her part.

I used Hypnosis and NLP with a follow-up session and foresee great results with the additional resources I now have.

Seta so far has improved on:

—her dance skills
—her feminine appearance
—her friendships (she no longer goes out of her way to please others as she used to)
—she is speaking out more about her feelings
—she looks happier, is constantly talking about and searching for her transformation and self-empowerment.

MY FAVORITE QUOTES

"Emotions are produced by our interpretations of the actions of others. What we feel is not based on our experience; it is based on our interpretation of that experience."
— Anthony Robbins

"It's fundamental to find our mission in life, in order to achieve happiness"
— Lygya Barreto

"I have enough money to last me the rest of my life unless I buy something."
— Jackie Mason

"Money is better than poverty, if only for financial reasons."
— Woody Allen

"When you go into court, you are putting your fate into the hands of twelve people who weren't smart enough to get out of jury duty."
— Norm Crosby

"Time waits for no one. Treasure every moment you have. You will treasure even more when you can share it with someone special—YOURSELF!"
—— Author Unknown

"If we judge people, we have no time to love them."
—— Mother Teresa

"If you think that something small ca not make a difference—try going to sleep with a mosquito in the room."
—— Author Unknown

"There are two ways to spread the light...
To be the candle or to be the mirror that reflects it..."
—— Edith Wharton

"Work like you don't need the money
Love like you've never been hurt
Dance like nobody is watching..."
—— Author Unknown

"Love humanity with you in it."
—— Author Unknown

NOTES

I agree with Daniel Goleman, when he wrote in his book *Emotional Intelligence* that a solution to or preventive strategy for, a lot of problems, could be emotional training and organization. Emotional management could be taught to children, to establish these processes as lifelong habits and to people reaching retirement age, as emotional well-being is one factor that determines whether an older person declines rapidly or thrives. He also mentions the third group of so-called "at-risk populations"—the very poor, single working mothers and residents of high-crime neighborhoods.

I add to this and say: "Every human being on this planet should be educated about thoroughly about their emotional experiences. To know why emotions exist, how to deal with them and what to do in order to heal them, it's necessary to place the subject on the curriculum of any institution, conference, seminar and media.

Knowledge is freedom if we learn how to be free...

Lygya B.

APPENDIX

The Four Levels of Healing & Creative Visualization—Shakti Gawain
Emotional Intelligence—Daniel Goleman
Getting Thru to Your Emotions with EFT—Phillip & Jane Mountrose
Our Evolution—Waldo Vieira
Anthony Robbins—Get the Edge
Stephen R. Covey—The 7 habits of Highly Effective People
Ted Andrews—How to Heal with Color

Have fun learning about life !!! Be a lovennaire!

—— Lygya Barreto

☺

Let me know about you at: **www.dearemotions.com**
Toll Free # 1(877) 866-1890

*Some exercises and explanations were inspired by Anthony Robbins Get The Edge coaching program. Highly recommended.

0-595-24698-2

www.ingramcontent.com/pod-product-compliance
Lightning Source LLC
Chambersburg PA
CBHW061305280526
45784CB00002B/895